paint
Ideas & Decorating Techniques

Better Homes and Gardens® Books
Des Moines, Iowa

Better Homes and Gardens® Books
An imprint of Meredith® Books

Paint Ideas & Decorating Techniques
Editor: Linda Hallam
Contributing Editors: Heather Lobdell, Elaine Markoutsas
Art Director: Jerry J. Rank
Decorative Painters/Stylists: Patty Kramer, Wade Scherrer
Copy Chief: Catherine Hamrick
Copy and Production Editor: Terri Fredrickson
Contributing Copy Editor: Jennifer Miller Mitchell
Contributing Proofreaders: Dan Degen, Margaret Smith, JoEllyn Witke
Indexer: Kathleen Poole
Electronic Production Coordinator: Paula Forest
Editorial and Design Assistants: Kaye Chabot, Mary Lee Gavin,
  Karen Schirm
Production Director: Douglas M. Johnston
Book Production Managers: Pam Kvitne, Marjorie J. Schenkelberg

Meredith® Books
Editor in Chief: James D. Blume
Design Director: Matt Strelecki
Managing Editor: Gregory H. Kayko
Executive Shelter Editor: Denise L. Caringer

Director, Sales & Marketing, Retail: Michael A. Peterson
Director, Sales & Marketing, Special Markets: Rita McMullen
Director, Sales & Marketing, Home & Garden Center Channel: Ray Wolf
Director, Operations: George A. Susral

Vice President, General Manager: Jamie L. Martin

Better Homes and Gardens® Magazine
Editor in Chief: Jean LemMon
Executive Interior Design Editor: Sandra S. Soria

Meredith Publishing Group
President, Publishing Group: Christopher M. Little
Vice President, Consumer Marketing & Development: Hal Oringer

Meredith Corporation
Chairman and Chief Executive Officer: William T. Kerr

Chairman of the Executive Committee: E. T. Meredith III

Cover Photograph: Peter Krumhardt. The room shown is on pages 24-25.

All of us at Better Homes and Gardens® Books are dedicated to providing you with information and ideas to enhance your home. We welcome your comments and suggestions. Write to us at: Better Homes and Gardens® Books, Shelter Editorial Department, 1716 Locust St., Des Moines, IA 50309-3023.

If you would like to purchase any of our books, check wherever quality books are sold. Visit our website at bhgbooks.com or bhg.com.

contents

getting started

Paint is the quickest, most economical way to decorate. With fresh color, you can quickly and economically **change the mood** of a room, or even your whole house. And when you add easy-to-learn decorative painting to your do-it-yourself repertoire, you have the techniques to **translate your imagination and creativity** into your own personal interiors. Use **part one** of this book, the first five chapters, to see how paint finishes look in room settings, and to learn to decorate your home with their beauty and charm. You'll see the standard and the latest techniques and learn how they complement today's popular decorating styles. Turn to **part two**, starting on page 105, for the **step-by-step photographs, techniques, and tips** that show you how to create them in your own color choices and settings.

If you are just **getting started** in the fascinating world of decorative painting, begin by creating a focal-point wall with basic techniques, such as the simplest sponging or ragging options. When you've mastered **basic techniques**, it's fun to learn slightly more advanced finishes, such as stylish striping or combing. With minor technique and tool changes, striping, combing, ragging, and sponging can be appropriate in both casual rooms and more dressy settings. You can find **the right look for your home**, decorating style, and skill level. You'll also see how special techniques make the most nondescript **rooms come alive**.

For an **inspiring start**, turn to Chapter One to learn how three homeowners **planned** their very different interiors around decorative finishes. Learn their

secrets about how to **tastefully** incorporate multiple finishes. Turn to chapters two through four for a room-by-room approach when you'd like to get started on a special project. Find **finishes that enliven** living and dining rooms, create restful bedrooms, and perk up kitchens and home offices. Each photograph is labeled with the name of the finish and refers to the page of the step-by-step technique. **Before you begin a project**, read the advice from skilled decorative painters on pages 106 and 107. Their suggestions and tips will help you work with the scale of your room and your furnishings. Each project lists materials, which are available at home centers, discount stores with paint departments, and hardware stores. Projects are based on water-based interior latex paint.

paint schemes that easily and tastefully complement interior styles. If you love vintage furniture and collections, you'll be inspired by paint finishes from the turn-of-the-century townhouse, pictured on *pages 10 through 19*. To avoid overwhelming the architecture, the owners used variations of one basic aging technique for the stairwell and the downstairs rooms. Colors ranging from a mellowed gold tone to a warm terra-cotta to a greenish parchment create interest. Upstairs, for a sitting room off the open stairwell, they chose to work with a suede finish in an olive green. The green is in a shade compatible with decorative golden accessories and the aged fresco finish of an adjoining wall.

wholehousecolor

Whatever the age and style of your home, consider the whole house when you plan your color and paint finish schemes.

NO MATTER THE STYLE OF YOUR HOUSE, you'll have vistas where you see two or more spaces at once. So it's important to consider how colors flow and decorative finishes complement each other. It's also important to remember that every room and every surface can't be the focal point. For decorative finishes to be interesting and tasteful, limit your techniques and showcased colors, and plan for plain, painted walls. These neutral spaces will make the decoratively painted walls all the more visually exciting.

This chapter illustrates three decorative

If your goal is a cottage style, turn to the small house with big style on *pages 20 through 27*. Working with a painter friend and a handy neighbor, the owner chose a linen technique for the living room and a moiré stripe for the dining room. For a change of mood, consider the contemporary townhouse on *pages 28 through 35*. Decorative paint finishes, chosen as part of a whole-house palette, create a backdrop for Asian art. This personal palette, a project done by the owner and a decorative painter, illustrates how multiple paint finishes can highlight without overwhelming when colors and techniques are chosen with care.

Before you choose your paint finishes and colors, assess the architectural style and detailing of your home.

UpdatedTraditional

FADED FRESCO VARIATION, *opposite*, in the living room, emulates the look of warm, sun-washed colors of aged stucco. The technique resembles old-world garden and terrace walls. The stairwell finish replicates the faded fresco with more visible brush strokes. **See pages 108–109 for technique.**

FADED FRESCO VARIATION, *above*, in the living room, brightens a room with decorative woodwork and a mix of fine antiques and rich fabrics. **See pages 108–109 for technique.**

YOU'LL BE HAPPIEST WITH THE RESULTS WHEN YOU PLAN DECORATIVE painting as a part of the overall interior design. Here, a restored late 19th century townhouse offered period detailing, including trim, moldings, and a handsome mantel. The owners have a fine and ever-changing collection of antique furnishings, art, and artifacts. In this setting, they chose the faded fresco technique to give the walls of the entry and stairwell the patina of aged plaster.

Because they like the aged-plaster look for the main rooms, they chose a variation of the same technique but altered the colors from mellow gold tones of the entry and stairwell wall to a warm terra-cotta for the formal living room. The warm tones brighten a dark entry and stairwell and play off the salvaged newel post and balusters. The shade also creates a stunning backdrop for collected antique tables, art, and interesting accessories and finds.

The terra-cotta color repeats the colors of a plaid silk chair and the decorative trim of the living room. At the same time, the flattering hue lightens a room of darker furnishings that include a leather sofa and decorative accent table. The red-based terra-cotta color of the traditionally furnished living room is balanced by the more neutral tones of the dining room color.

In the adjacent dining room, the parchment with green adds a subtle walled-garden effect

FADED FRESCO VARIATION, *opposite*, in the living room, blends with the dining room's rolling and ragging finish. **See pages 108–109 for technique.**

FADED FRESCO VARIATION, *upper left*, enriches plain walls with the depth of color and layers of texture. **See pages 108–109 for technique.**

FADED FRESCO, *upper right*, works well with stylish faded colors. **See pages 108–109 for technique.**

ROLLING AND RAGGING, *lower left*, a color washed technique, creates an excellent backdrop for casually elegant interiors and furnishings. Choose lighter shades for interest. **See pages 110–111 for technique.**

ROLLING AND RAGGING, *lower right*, lightens the look of traditional dark wood and tapestries. The finish contrasts equally well with bold and graphic contemporary art. **See pages 110–111 for technique.**

to urn prints and urns on pedestals. A European candle chandelier above the carved table carries the decorating themes of the handsome and casually sophisticated room.

Upstairs, walls with a suede-type finish warm the sitting and television room used particularly during the cool-weather months. The deep green is also a handsome contrast to the gold-hued walls of the open, gallery-like stairwell. The green provides a stunning backdrop for additional art and a French fruitwood armoire and a Bombay chest. For a more lighthearted vein for the remodeled bath, the owners used a technique of blending spots of paint on a white background. And for the decorative walls of the home office, they chose a muted sunset pink variation of the faded fresco finish.

FADED FRESCO, *above left,* looks best when the colors are kept fairly light. The final color wash gives depth and character to standard drywall. **See pages 108–109 for technique.**

SUEDE, *above right,* adds texture and the look of a beautiful sheen with a specially formulated paint that's sold under several brand names. The technique lends an air of sophistication to interiors. **See pages 126–127 for technique.**

FADED FRESCO, *opposite,* replicates the look of time-worn plaster with a subtle technique that's an ideal backdrop. Since the technique adds the illusion of depth, faded fresco works well for walls that display art and collections, such as the grouping of a framed quilt and carved masks shown here. **See pages 108–109 for technique.**

 **BLENDED SPOTS**, *opposite,* add interest and
depth to a small space, such as the bathroom shown
here. The look is loosely based on marbleizing or
feathering finishes but is easier to accomplish. Neutral
colors, with only brighter colors used as accents, work
best as the technique—rather than the colors—gives
the interest. **See pages 112–113 for technique.**

 **BLENDED SPOTS**, *above,* are ideal for
half-wall situations, such as above the beaded-board
wainscoting, as a little goes a long way with graphic
techniques. The spots combine with the whitewashing
over wood. **See pages 112–113 for technique.**

FADED FRESCO, *above,* is subtle enough for areas such as this home office. Consider how techniques and paint colors contrast or blend with your trim and flooring. **See pages 108–109 for technique.**

FADED FRESCO, *opposite,* blends easily from room to room and provides a handsome, serene backdrop for furnishings. When you base color changes on furnishings, fabrics, and art, the differences between rooms can be noticeable enough to be interesting. **See pages 108–109 for technique.**

CottageStyle

Pretty colors, such as sunny yellows, and cheerful techniques create the mood of a year-round summer cottage.

WHEN YOU ARE THINKING ABOUT PAINTING TWO OR MORE ROOMS WITH DECORATIVE TECHNIQUES, varying the tints of your favorite color and including plain, painted spaces is an easy way to avoid too much of a good thing. In this country cottage in the city, the owner chose pale yellow for a pretty, feminine living room. The linen finish, which is a variation of vertical and horizontal combing, is subdued enough to add interest without competing with the decorative transom and vintage-style furnishings that enrich the room. Rather than contrasting or competing with the walls, the unlined, yellow gauze cotton window treatments simply soften the light and add privacy. Together, the fabric and the curvy French-style sofa and chair provide a pretty, traditional counterpoint to the summery painted-linen wall treatment.

The yellow dining room, furnished with American country pieces, features striped moiré walls. The background color is more intense than the linen finish to allow clearly visible contrast with the combed stripes. The 3-inch-wide stripes give the room a lighthearted ambience that updates the country furnishings. As calming, neutral space between the rooms, the entry is a soothing, mint green. Here, walls are plain, allowing the living and dining rooms to be the stars of the newly restored cottage. When multiple rooms feature decorative techniques, plan areas with plain, painted walls. Choose colors that complement the decoratively painted spaces.

LINEN, *opposite,* replicates the look of fabric because the painting is done in a "weaving" technique with a special brush. For the light, open feel of linen fabrics, choose a summery shade such as this sunny yellow to brighten vintage living room furnishings. Consider fabric, such as these window treatments, in a deeper tone to reinforce your color scheme. The linen technique also infuses bedrooms and sunrooms with stylish, relaxed appeal. **See pages 116–117 for technique and page 160 for sources.**

LINEN, *opposite,* recalls the light, woven texture, with noticeable warp and weft. Because of the subtlety of the technique, it's ideal for this cottage setting. Colors in the range of natural linens also work well with the sleek lines of contemporary, upholstered pieces. The backdrop is a suitable one for art because the technique doesn't compete with paintings.
See pages 116–117 for technique and page 160 for sources.

LINEN, *above,* is a good choice when you are looking for a paint technique to update your furniture and accessories. Here, the youthful look lightens and brightens a room once weighed down with dark, painted walls. For best results, enlist a partner and allow three days for proper drying time. Your time and effort will be rewarded with an appealing, lighthearted look.
See pages 116–117 for technique and page 160 for sources.

SOLID GREEN, *above,* illustrates the importance of plain, painted spaces when you use decorative techniques, such as the dining room's moiré stripes, as focal points. Vary the colors for interest and to create a definite demarcation. Choose the sheen of your plain paint finish to complement the adjoining decorative finishes. For example, if decoratively painted walls are flat, a flat finish will be complementary for the neutral spaces.

MOIRÉ STRIPES, *opposite,* give a stylized interpretation of moiré, a textured woven fabric. In this dining room, the choice creates a nice complement to the painted-linen technique that enlivens the cottage's living room. As with the linen, lighter pastel tints of colors work best to keep the look from overwhelming. The happy yellow also highlights the owner's collection of vintage and new art pottery. **See pages 114–115 for technique.**

MOIRÉ STRIPES, *opposite*, update the dining room and its country oak pieces with lively color and pattern. When you plan to work with multiple paint techniques, choose one to stand out so your rooms don't compete with each other. Painted stripes enrich with the look of texture and pattern and are ideal for rooms where the walls can be the decorative stars. **See pages 114–115 for technique.**

MOIRÉ STRIPES, *upper left,* are an example of how an interesting technique can invigorate a collection of vintage furniture and art. **See pages 114–115 for technique.**

MOIRÉ STRIPES, *upper right, lower left, and lower right,* were chosen to work with the colors and textures of the owner's table linens, glassware, and collections. When you plan a color scheme and complementary technique, consider how your backdrop will reflect your furnishings. Here, the texture highlights collected pottery, while the wide stripe reinforces the solid feel of the country oak furniture. **See pages 114–115 for technique.**

Far East **Suburban**

When you move or decide to redecorate, seize the opportunity to create a home that reflects your interests and color preferences.

IF YOUR WALLS ARE PLAIN WHITE AND YOUR FLOORING NEUTRAL, CONSIDER THEM A CLEAN SLATE FOR A NEW BEGINNING. Start with the positives of what you love and open your imagination to the possibilities of an innovative color palette and decorative paint finishes. As a first step, think about how much light your rooms receive and the effects of flooring and woodwork on color choices. Concentrate your decorative finishes as accent walls for larger, open rooms—particularly those with vaulted or unusually high ceilings. Save overall specialty finishes for rooms of standard size and ceiling height, and more intricate finishes for smaller focal points. When you are decorating several rooms at one time, choose a finish appropriate to the mood and use of each room.

This suburban townhouse is an illustrative case in point with its vaulted ceiling and open space. The owner successfully used a variety of paint finishes to define the moods of rooms used for different purposes. The project began with the owner's collection of Asian art and his interest in the Far East. New upholstered pieces, chosen to work with the art, set the color scheme for the vaulted living room that opens to the stairwell and the dine-

DOUBLE-ROLLED, *opposite,* creates a focal point for architecture, art, and collections. In this townhouse, the two rolled colors transform a standard mantel into a gallery-like setting for the owner's Asian art. **See pages 118–119 for technique.**

DOUBLE-ROLLED, *right,* repeats the tones of the art, such as the masks, but with enough variations for contrast and texture. **See pages 118–119 for technique.**

in kitchen. The colors also carry over to the home office and the powder room.

Because of the sheer amount of wall space, the owner first planned the background walls that would not be decoratively finished. He chose a warm, neutral tan that would work throughout and wisely started with the living room, the largest and most visible room of the two-story townhouse. Instead of a piecemeal approach, he planned the palette for the whole house so the colors and finishes play off each other and highlight his art. In the living room, the natural focal point of the fireplace takes on more importance with a rolled finish that emulates the textured colors of dried leaves. This backdrop frames a mantel arrangement of carved masks and pottery.

The adjacent kitchen, visible from the entry and living room, features two shades of green to blend with favorite Japanese prints. The wall below the chair rail is combed in a creamy linen color over the deeper green. Such accent walls are ideal for combing, a handsome but fairly painstaking technique.

SOLID TAN, *above left,* provides the crucial neutral space in a townhouse with six decorative paint finishes. Decorative finishes can be overpowering in areas with vaulted ceilings and large expanses of wall space. Instead, take advantage of the luxury of open space for a gallery display.

SOLID TAN, *above right,* blends with the colors of fabrics and accessories as well as decorative finishes.

SOLID GREEN AND COMBING, *opposite,* play off each other to add visual design interest to the townhouse's informal dining area. Combing is easy to do with the proper tools and is effective in small spaces. Here, combing creates the look of wainscoting below the chair rail. The framed Japanese prints inspired the moss green color choice. **See pages 120–121 for combing technique.**

To give the other main downstairs room the character of a library retreat, the owner decided on a leather-type technique in shades of aged gold. Handsome in its own right, the finish brightens a room that receives little daylight and complements the oak woodwork. The adjacent red powder room highlights carved masks.

Upstairs, two favorite shades of blue and two finishes set the schemes for the master bedroom and meditation room. Bedroom walls are painted with commercially available, suede-finish paint. The meditation room, planned to emulate the serenity of a Far East garden, appears as though walls are covered with sheer chambray cloth. Instead, they are painted with a combination of horizontal and vertical dragging.

And in the pièce de résistance, the upstairs bath features all the colors in the palette, except red, painted as a sporty, tailored plaid.

LEATHER, *opposite,* ages new spaces, such as this townhouse's home office. The technique is ideal for rooms with a library look and feel. Here, a golden leather tone energizes a room with dark oak furniture and little natural light. **See pages 122–123 for technique and page 160 for sources.**

SOLID RED, *above,* illustrates the appeal of an interesting color for rooms that serve as balances to decorative finishes. If you are unused to strong color, consider one for a small area such as this stylish bath.

PLAID, *left,* recalls the popular woven fabric. The technique is based on simple sponging but requires careful measuring. Choose the technique for rooms, such as this windowless bath, where a small area can yield large decorative impact. Here, the plaid uses most of the colors in the townhouse's color palette. **See pages 152–155 for technique.**

CHAMBRAY, *opposite,* recalls the woven texture of the classic work shirt fabric. The technique is related to linen as it is created with specialty brushes, which are sold in kits. Here, in a cool blue color, the technique reflects the calm of a meditation room with Far Eastern influences. The technique would translate well into a charming bedroom when paired with white furnishings. **See pages 124–125 for technique and page 160 for sources.**

CHAMBRAY, *top,* relaxes a small, private room used for meditation. Soft colors work best for this low-key finish. **See pages 124–125 for technique and page 160 for sources.**

SUEDE, *bottom,* adds texture, through a specially formulated paint, to plain walls. Here, the owner chose blue for a peaceful bedroom that adjoins his meditation room. The two blues blend without competing. **See pages 126–127 for technique and page 160 for sources.**

living&dining

Whatever your style, look, mood, or color preference, you'll find a decorative paint finish that enhances your living and dining areas. Consider how you want your rooms to feel and the colors of your furnishings. If you are updating a room with existing fabrics, you have the option of working with a similar wall color in a fresh technique or starting anew with a revised scheme. For example, if your existing walls are yellow, repeat yellow–but in a new linen or striped finish. Perhaps you are ready for a change and want to switch from yellow to terra-cotta in a sponged finish. If you are getting started with decorative painting, you may want to experiment with a focal point wall in a room. Or you may want to try the effect only in your entry or above a chair rail.

For the best results with your choices, match the decorative finish to the style of your room. Techniques, such as strié, which emulate traditional fabrics or wallpapers, lend themselves to more formal settings. Other techniques, such as the ever-classic sponging or ragging, work well for a variety of styles. Generally, the looser the strokes, the more informal the effect. The trend today for country-, cottage-, and garden-style rooms are the aged techniques, which recall the effects of time-worn plaster. The smoke-stain technique, shown on pages 36 and 37, gives an ideal background for country furnishings.

living&dining

Balance a colorful, decorative wall finish with the relief of white woodwork and solid upholstery fabric.

SPONGING, *opposite,* works well in most settings, depending on how paint is applied and the colors chosen. Decorative painters often adhere to the rule that the looser and more open the sponging, the more casual the look. Here, a persimmon color is densely sponged over a paler background color. The decorator chose the color to blend with the antique rug and the tapestry fabrics. Choose closely related colors to avoid jarring contrasts. **See pages 138–139 for technique.**

GLAZE OVER PAINT, *below,* enriches plain walls with depth and sheen. The technique uses commercial glaze, which can be tinted or purchased pretinted. Choose a glazed backdrop for rooms where accessories and furnishings, rather than a decorative technique, create interest. The shine from glaze creates sparkle in rooms used primarily in the evening. Professional decorators glaze vivid wall colors for drama and background for beautiful fabrics and furnishings. Glazing also highlights stylish pale or neutral walls.

STRIÉ, *opposite,* creates a tailored backdrop for a traditionally furnished living room. Based on a dragging technique, strié is effective in living and dining rooms and entries of varying sizes. Base your color choice on the setting and the mood you are designing. In more traditional living and dining rooms, deep jewel tones—such as emerald or bottle green, royal blue, or deep red—are pleasing choices. Strié also combines well with plain or papered walls when it's used above or below a chair rail. In more contemporary rooms, strié presents subtle backdrop when neutral colors are used. **See pages 136–137 for technique.**

SMOKED STAIN OVER RAGGING OFF, *above,* combines two techniques to re-create the look of years of natural aging. Such aged finishes are a suitable background for distressed furniture and are popular for decorating schemes based on country furnishings and collectibles. **See pages 128–129 for technique.**

SMOKED STAIN OVER RAGGING OFF, *right,* amplifies with the earthy colors of country decorating. More noticeably "stained" areas, created with tinted glaze, look best where they would naturally occur, such as in corners between walls and around woodwork and trim. **See pages 128–129 for technique.**

● **COLOR WASHED OVER PLASTERED BRICK**, *above,* adds interest to a contemporary living room. The technique enhances the texture of the brick so that the fireplace wall balances the roughness of the sisal rug and bench. Decorative finishes introduce texture without color. **See pages 108–109 for color washing (faded fresco) technique.**

● **SPONGING**, *opposite,* over stippling, doesn't overwhelm a room with deep windows and light carpet and furniture. Stipple first, allow to dry, then sponge. In a room with less light, choose paler shades for the wall. **See page 123, direction A, for stippling techique; see pages 138–139 for sponging technique.**

GLAZING OVER SPONGED STRIPES, *opposite,* gives a hand-painted interpretation of classic, striped wallpaper. When art and furniture are the focal points in a room, choose subtle colors from tints on the same paint card. Neutral colors translate well into this stylish, relaxed look. Consider the impact of jewel-tone stripes for a living or dining room used primarily at night. **See pages 134–135 for stripes technique.**

WIDE STRIPES, *upper left,* set an interesting, welcoming tone for a foyer. The finish highlights pieces such as this gilded chair and framed print—and visually expands a small space. Choose colors that blend harmoniously with adjoining rooms. **See pages 134–135 for stripes technique.**

RAGGING OFF, *upper right,* introduces the element of dimension. Paint is rolled on, then removed with rags. The result gives a hint of pleasing texture without competing with collections. Darker shades, as shown here, or lighter tints, can be ragged off. **See pages 128–129 for technique.**

TAPED AND DOUBLE-ROLLED, *left,* turns a blank wall into a room's focal point. Use a cardboard square, level, and ruler to mark off squares. Mask off with low-tack painter's tape. Note the repetition of shapes in the caned-back chair for pleasing visual rhythm. Choose colors that meld without sharp contrast. **See pages 118–119 for double-rolled technique.**

living&**dining**

Color-washed neutral colors translate blank walls and ceilings into rooms that relax formal furnishings.

COLOR WASHED WITH DILUTED PAINT, *opposite*, recreates the appeal of old fresco without textured paints or glazes. This popular look ages new construction. Dilute white latex paint with water and color wash the ceiling and walls. Shades of cream and brown soften the effects. **See pages 108–109 for color wash (faded fresco).**

COLOR WASHED WITH DILUTED PAINT, *left,* sets the color tones for graceful window treatments in a rich silk fabric. The ceiling could be lightened or darkened for more dramatic contrast. **See pages 108–109 for color wash (faded fresco).**

COMBED COLOR WASH AND SPONGING, *opposite,* takes advantage of the chair rail to combine two treatments. Above the chair rail, the color wash is combed for texture. Below, sponging creates the contrast of wainscoting. The darker color anchors the room. **See pages 108–109 for color wash (faded fresco); pages 120–121 for combing; and pages 138–139 for sponging.**

TINTED TEXTURED PAINT, *top right,* uses a commercially available paint to recreate the look and feel of stucco. The colors, here warm yellow with tints of ochre, are added to the paint. If you prefer to add texture to walls, recreate the look with ragging or ragging off techniques.

DIAMOND PATTERN, *bottom right,* translates the classic look of traditional 12-inch-square tile floors to a decorative painted finish. To avoid overdecorating a more formal living room, keep wall and window treatments simple when the floor works as such a strong design element. The repetition of the diamond shape on the painted chest and the graphic fabric tie the look together. **See pages 156–159 for technique.**

STRIPES (FLAT PAINT), *above,* introduce variations of neutral color into a monochromatic, contemporary dining room. Stripes warm such serene rooms without the impact of vivid color or busy pattern. The color blends with the carpet and the natural wood furniture. If you prefer more contrast between stripes, paint semigloss stripes over a flat wall finish. Or choose the lightest and darkest colors on a paint chip card. Two- to three-inch-wide stripes are a pleasing scale for average-size dining or living rooms. **See pages 134–135 for stripes technique.**

SPONGED STRIPES, *opposite,* create the illusion of higher ceiling height. Here, the verticality of the stripes combine with the window treatments hung below the molding to give a standard dining room an open, airy feel. To make a room feel larger, choose light colors with a noticeable, but not pronounced, contrast between the stripes. Decide which element in your room will be the star. The quiet wall colors allow the antique rug and the chandelier to be the decorating focal points. **See pages 134–135 for stripes technique; see pages 138–139 for sponging technique.**

FAUX-TILE FLOOR, *below,* transforms a small dining area and basic furnishings into a European-inspired setting. To disguise a worn floor, the owners painted a decorative faux-tile motif. With the floor as the anchor of the sunny scheme, walls are color washed with diluted latex paint in the warm yellows associated with Country French colors. When two techniques are combined, keep one simple for a pleasing effect. **See pages 146–147 for faux-tile technique; see pages 108–109 for color wash (faded fresco).**

RANDOM COMBING, *opposite,* demonstrates the impact of a well-chosen finish for a contemporary interior. The aubergine color imparts drama that's heightened by the random combing. The color and pattern effectively frame the graphic prints. The best rule to follow when color and technique are involved? The more dramatic the color, the simpler the finish. **See pages 114–115 for combing (moiré stripes) technique; see pages 120–121 for standard combing technique.**

bed&bath

Bedrooms—more than ever private retreats—are ideal places to calm down or spruce up with special paint finishes. To make a bedroom and bath your own, choose a technique and color scheme that reflects your taste and furnishings. Bedrooms lend themselves to everything from the softest sponging to the newer techniques that emulate fabrics, suedes, and leathers. Stripes, diamonds, or hand-painted squares are options for lively, current looks. If you enjoy the popular aged look, consider the ragging techniques that recall old stucco walls.

Be equally imaginative for a child's room or nursery. Painted in fashionable bright pastels, stripes and diamonds translate into lighthearted backgrounds for art and window treatments. Or try your hand at easy freehand designs with stripes and flowers in charming motifs and colors. Remember the quick-change effects of paint for less-than-perfect floors. When you are redoing a bedroom, a checkerboard pattern can be the final finishing touch.

If you are just starting decorative painting, or if you want to learn new techniques, baths and powder rooms provide ideal venues. These smaller rooms come to life with color and painted pattern. Besides the sponged technique—applied with cellulose kitchen sponges—in this chapter, you'll want to review the stylish plaid and the arty blended spots techniques in Chapter One.

bed&bath

Choose paint colors and techniques that unify your existing furnishings and enhance the decorating look you enjoy. Softer colors and simple finishes relax bedroom schemes.

STRIPES, *opposite,* relax the formality of decorative French-style furniture. For a lighthearted feel, visually "tent" the ceiling with hand-painted stripes. Choose soft, subtle colors with minimal contrast. **See pages 134–135 for technique.**

STRIPES, *above,* fit the corners and angles of attic-like spaces. Think blending, rather than exactly matching colors, when you are pairing painted stripes with painted furniture and cheerfully printed floral fabrics. **See pages 134–135 for technique.**

STREAKY SQUARES, *opposite,* warm plain walls with a look that resembles hand-cut stone. For the most pleasing setting, limit the technique to larger rooms with higher ceilings that won't be overpowered by the squares. Choose natural colors, such as tans or light sandstone colors, that are representative of stones in nature. Here, the scale works well as the backdrop for reproduction engravings and an oversize, padded leather bed. The grid of squares sets up an interesting counterpoint to the bed's sophisticated curves. **See pages 132–133 for technique.**

CHECKERBOARD, *below,* updates a worn wood floor in an attic bedroom. Depending on your preference, tape the painted floor for squares as shown, or turn squares at a 45-degree angle for a diamond pattern. Choose the floor colors and finishes to be compatible with the walls and furnishings of your bedroom. To visually anchor a room, select a darker shade of the wall color for one of the floor colors. The contrasting color can be the white, off-white, or stained wood, as shown here, depending on your scheme and preference. Painted floors should always be finished with matte-finish polyurethane to stand up to normal wear. **See pages 156–159 for technique.**

HAND-PAINTED DIAMONDS, *opposite,* translate a technique based on measuring and drawing into a spirited wall treatment that's ideal for a child's or teen's room. For a youthful, playful mood, choose white, a pale pastel, or a neutral for the background and a lively, brighter pastel for the diagonal stripes. Circles, made by tracing coins, allow you to introduce additional color accents. The treatment works well in rooms with other painted pieces, as colors can be repeated. And it's fun, too, as a trellis-style backdrop for hanging art, accessories, and small, decorative plates. **See pages 150–151 for technique.**

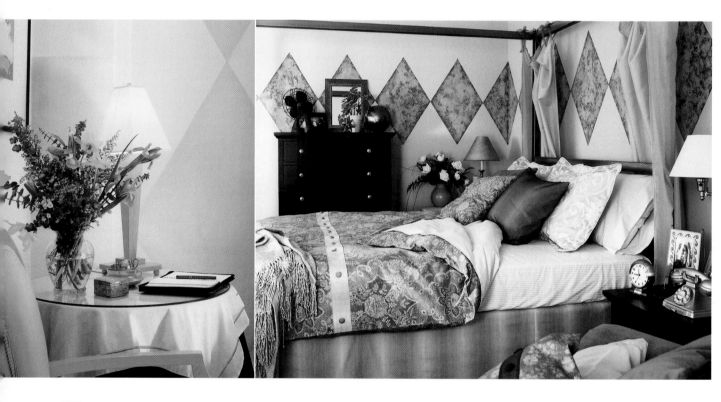

LARGE DIAMOND PATTERN (PAINTED), *above left,* lends a sophisticated air to rooms decorated with contemporary furniture and art. When furniture is in simple, graphic shapes, choose oversize diamonds to avoid too much pattern or unsettling contrast. Soft colors can be distressed with a color wash to age the look. Measure so that diamonds are properly spaced. Consider the technique for a focal-point wall, rather than an entire room. Paint adjoining walls in one of the colors. **See pages 150–151 for diamond technique.**

LARGE-SCALE DIAMOND PATTERN (RAGGING OFF), *above right,* combines the drama of diamonds with the visual texture of ragging off. The design interest comes from the unexpected pairing of cool, metallic blue with warm, natural browns. The ragging repeats the textures of the tailored linen bedskirt and the woven damask duvet color. If you prefer less contrast, the technique can be executed in two colors from the same paint card. Or the ragging could be replaced by subtler sponging. **See pages 150–151 for diamond technique.**

STRIÉ, *opposite,* details a traditionally furnished bedroom with the look of a classic wallpaper or fine fabric. Here, the soothing dark green repeats the green leaves of the floral print. Open-background, light fabrics lend a note of visual contrast that allow such a dark color to calm, rather than overwhelm, a room. **See pages 136–137 for strié technique.**

COMBING, *top right,* refines the background in a room of icy pastels. The texture contrasts with the smoothness of collected white porcelains that are arranged and hung as art. Such combed finishes can be used effectively above wainscoting, as shown, for the effect of wallpaper. Lighter wall colors introduce a feeling of summer when combined with white woodwork and white or pale fabrics. **See pages 120–121 for combing technique.**

COMBED, *bottom right,* hints at color and texture in a serene bedroom retreat. For a quiet, peaceful ambience, choose pale colors in neutrals or light pastels. This versatile technique in shades of palest taupe, gray, or off-white works well in settings, such as this room, where one furniture piece punctuates with color. Consider a neutral, textural, combed finish in contemporary settings when large pieces of vibrant art set the decorating mood. **See pages 120–121 for combing technique.**

STRIPES, *above left,* illustrate the pretty, always-classic color combination of blue and white. Here, the blue is a cool, stylish periwinkle that lends itself well to a teenager's bedroom. The stripes provide a lively counterpoint to the woven coverlet hung as art above the bed. A horizontal, pleated window treatment adds the design interest of contrasting lines. When a room is likely to change, choose such classic color combinations and decorative techniques. The versatile striped walls, which seem old fashioned with the mix of vintage furnishings, fabrics, and white wicker, could feel equally sporty or contemporary with a quick change of furniture, linens, and window treatments. **See pages 134–135 for stripes technique.**

STRIPES, *above center,* take on a sophisticated, grown-up flair in a luxurious master bedroom. For this look, choose two shades of rich gold that blend with an equally opulent woven fabric for the padded, shirred headboard and duvet cover. The repetition of colors in the painted stripes and fabrics enrich the setting. For a cooler look, decorate with shades of silver, off-white, or pale tans. **See pages 134–135 for stripes technique.**

● **COLOR BLOCK STRIPES**, *above right,* perk up a small guest room with wide bands of copper-color textured paint, tempered by two colors of flat green paint. First, paint the walls with the lightest color of flat paint; then mark off stripes with a level and straightedge; pencil in guidelines. Mask off and roll on the bands of the darker flat paint; allow to dry. Mask off and roll on textured paint. Stripes here are 6, 12, 18, and 30 inches wide. Purchase the sand-textured paint at home centers and larger paint stores. For the most effective backdrop, choose colors of noticeable contrast but with similar brightness, as shown here. Two neutral colors from the same paint card pair well with a more dramatic color.

FLOWER BORDER, *below left,* decorates a young girl's attic-style bedroom with a happy, '60s-inspired daisy motif. Select lively, fresh colors to have fun with such easy, freehand techniques. The secret to the look is carefully taping and measuring the border and casually brushing on the background. **See pages 142–143 for technique.**

TAPED STRIPES, *below right,* give a crisp, youthful background to painted furniture when a vivid green pairs with bright white. **See pages 140–141 for technique.**

FLOWER BORDER, *opposite top,* repeats the stylized daisy motif of the duvet cover. Look for such graphic motifs that can be translated into hand-painted borders. The naive, less-than-perfect look contributes to the charm of hand painting. Borders decorate a room without the time and expense of an overall wall technique. Paint trim in one of the border colors. **See pages 142–143 for technique.**

TAPED STRIPES, *opposite bottom,* tent a girl's room in circus style. Wider stripes, here 3 inches, lend an informal, playful air to a bedroom. Base your stripe color on a fabric or other color in your room. Here, a cotton chair slipcover inspires the lively, stylish green paired with always-crisp white. For a softer look with stripes, decorate with two shades of yellow or a pale yellow and cream. **See pages 140–141 for technique.**

SPONGING, *opposite,* tints a plain wall with hints of warm color. As with ragginging, the looser the sponging, the more informal the look and feel of a room. Here, in a country-style room, walls are loosely sponged as a backdrop to painted woodwork and colorful fabrics. As the vintage fabrics, rug, and furnishings set the scheme, the sponging gives subtle contrast but is a background player. Choose techniques and colors that enhance, rather than overwhelm, your room. **See pages 138-139 for sponging technique.**

RAGGING, *right,* enriches a bedroom with earthy tones. The density of the ragging imparts a more formal look to the setting and a handsome palette for framed mirrors. The look of ragging varies, depending on the material chosen for the rags. Cotton rags translate into a blended look, as does minimal contrast. **See pages 110–111; 128–129; and 150–151 for variations of ragging techniques.**

SPONGING, *left,* introduces soft shades of creamy white into a pretty yellow bedroom. Lightly sponge in colors from the same paint chip card to avoid harsh contrast. Choose yellows and warm pinks when you want a warm, cozy feel. If you prefer a cool, serene retreat, sponge in shades of cool, pale blue or in lighter greens. Subtle sponging with a natural sponge contributes a quiet background that works with a variety of fabrics, such as the woven tapestry shown here. **See pages 138–139 for technique.**

HAND-PAINTED CLOUDS, *below,* quickly and easily impart an aerial theme to a boy's bedroom. Paint your child's room, including the ceiling, with flat latex paint in a shade of sky blue. Allow the paint to thoroughly dry. Use an artist's brush with a tapered tip and diluted white latex paint to delicately paint the puffy clouds. Vary the shapes, sizes, and configurations of the clouds for the most natural effect. Practice first on scrap boards to make sure you are satisfied with the look. (If the clouds appear heavy on the board, further dilute the paint.) With this blue and white beginning, introduce accents of red, such as the plaid upholstery and lamp bases here, for a sporty, All-American decorating scheme.

CROSS-HATCHED BORDER, *opposite,* uses one simple motion and a tapered artist's brush to create a decorative border. Although the charming style of the painted border is in its painterly look, measure down from the ceiling for dots that will guide you for the top of the border. You'll also want to determine, before you start, roughly how wide the cross-hatching should be for the most pleasing effect. Here, the crossed lines were planned slightly wider than the largest plate to serve as the visual base for the border. As with all techniques, practice first on scrap boards to make sure you are comfortable with this freehand technique. The secret to a pleasing look is to do the cross-hatching in a quick motion, starting at the top of each crossed line.

Paint—and jaunty stripes—dress up baths whether your style is
budget-conscious, country casual, or sleek contemporary.

bed&**bath**

STRIPES, *opposite,* energize a small, remodeled bath with cheerful yellow and creamy off-white.
The look here is casual and hand-painted, rather than precise, to meld with the relaxed charm of the
distressed, recycled vanity and vintage linens. (Try it for a child's room, too.) Semigloss paint works well for
baths, as it resists moisture and is easier than flat finishes to clean. **See pages 134–135 for technique.**

STRIPES, *above,* take on a glamorous feel in sophisticated shades of serene taupe. The combination
of semigloss and flat paint contrasts for shine and pleasing texture. Narrower, more precise stripes tend to
look dressier, as illustrated here, than wider ones. **See pages 134–135 for stripes technique.**

DIAMONDS, *opposite,* update time-worn, less-than-pristine walls with an engaging new finish. Rather than mask imperfections of aged plaster, the decorator simply measured, taped, and painted over the wall with the sophisticated diamond motif. Colors mimic the natural look of aged plaster. Decorative beads from a crafts store are glued at the points for finishing touches. In a larger room, restrict this much drama to a focal-point wall. **See pages 150–151 for diamond technique.**

PLAID, *upper left ,* decorates an upstairs bath in a new suburban house. The homeowner taped and painted horizontal bands for color. For the plaid effect, walls were retaped and rolled with diluted white latex paint.

STRIPES, *upper right,* impart a serene backdrop to a stylish powder room with hints of the Far East. For a quiet treatment, choose colors that are adjacent or only a position or two apart on a color card. Neutral colors or palest pastels are visually calm. **See pages 134–135 for stripes technique.**

SPONGE-STAMPED BRICK, *lower left,* illustrates the impact of sponging as stamping. Use this technique in rooms, such as small powder rooms or small entries, where texture as well as color contribute to the design. Choose accessories in blending or coordinating colors to strengthen the overall effect of the finish. **See pages 144–145 for technique.**

STENCILED COLOR BLOCKS, *below left,* update an old-fashioned bath with plain white walls. The technique involves a quick combination of cut-out poster board stencil, stencil adhesive to hold it in place, and spray paint. Cutouts are 3 inches square. For the most decorating impact, choose a lively accent color and repeat it in a key accent, such as the painted chair, and in bath linens. For a child's bath, a combination of primary colors or spirited pastels would be a fun and cheerful alternative.

RAGGING WITH STAMPING, *above right,* utilizes the basic technique of densely ragging with closely matching colors for a sophisticated backdrop. Rosy shades of terra-cotta were chosen to complement the saltillo tile countertop. For an extra touch of detail and glint of gold, the owners used a commercial stamp to add random fleur-de-lis motifs to the painted wall. Choose abstract graphic motifs and stamp randomly for the most pleasing look. **See pages 110–111; 128–129; and 150–151 for variations of ragging techniques.**

FAUX-TILE WALL, *opposite,* derives its charm from the freehand, painterly look. This lively scheme, based on 4-inch-square tiles, works well for children's bathrooms as it's playful and youthful but not babyish. An easy-to-choose combination pairs two colors, such as the blue and green shown here, that are near each other on the color wheel. If you prefer the dynamic mixing of opposites, such as orange and blue, choose colors of the same intensities (degree of brightness). **See faux-tile wall directions, pages 146–147.**

kitchens etc

These are the often the busiest rooms in your home. So why not make them the brightest and most welcoming for your family and friends? If you are new to decorative painting, an easy start is to pair the simpler sponging and ragging techniques with pretty, lively colors. Or for a dining bay, work with a technique such as combing below the chair rail. The amount of wall space and time involved will be small but the impact large. For extra fun, test your artistic abilities with the quick hand-painted vine technique in this chapter.

In these rooms with so much traffic and activity, avoid the specialty paints not suitable for high-moisture spaces. Instead, choose techniques and paints, such as semigloss latex finishes, that can be wiped clean. Floors, too, revive with cheerful, creative color combinations and techniques.

And whether your ideal office is an English library or a high-tech hideaway, set the scene with a decorative paint finish. The faux-leather and suede techniques, accomplished with glazes and specially formulated paints, re-create the rich, varied colors of fine furniture. Think of a leather sofa or a suede-covered easy chair to picture the subtle color variations and sophisticated shadings techniques of these finishes. As walls become art with these handsome techniques, little extra decoration is required to make a design statement.

kitchens etc.

Make a decorative finish in a favorite color part of your kitchen plan—whether you are sprucing up, remodeling, or building your dream home.

STRIPES, *right,* in soft neutrals set a stylish but not dominating tone for a kitchen decorated for entertaining and family living. Stripes amplify but don't distract in kitchens and breakfast rooms where the fabrics and collections are in the forefront. When you choose neutral colors, it's easy to achieve a new look or seasonal changes with quick switches of accessories. As a counterpoint to the stripes, unfinished wood cabinets in this kitchen were washed with diluted paint for subtle color that allows the grain of the wood to show. To achieve the effect, dilute latex paint with water and rub on with clean rags. **See pages 134–135 for stripes technique.**

STUCCO FINISH, *opposite,* enlivens a small, budget-conscious, dine-in kitchen with buckskin color and texture that warm the crisp black and white scheme. The finish, done with a specially formulated textured paint, works particularly well as the shelving stands out against visible wall space. **See page 160 for source.**

STUCCO FINISH, *above,* creates the backdrop for the combination of utilitarian and decorative elements. Repeat the wall color in several accessories, such as picture mats and bowls, to tie such an edited scheme together. **See page 160 for source.**

⬭ **STIPPLING**, *below,* bridges the design trends of vintage and high tech for kitchen remodelings. In an older home with a modern, commercial-grade kitchen, decorative walls repeat the deep colors of the restored home while introducing a note of texture and blending colors. Colors amplify the adjoining room and work with the copper range hood and granite countertops. Stippling is done as part of the leather technique. **See pages 122–123 for stippling (leather) technique.**

⬭ **STIPPLING**, *right,* in sun-drenched shades of gold recalls Italy and the South of France. The colors and technique meld for the inviting backdrop the owners wanted for a dining area furnished with a natural-fiber, outdoor-style woven table and chairs. The gold tones also contrast beautifully with the purple glass insets, as they are opposites on the color wheel. Select warm, rich shades of blending colors when your goal is to energize a room. Simple furnishings stand out against such backgrounds. **See pages 122–123 for stippling (leather) technique.**

CHECKERBOARD ON DIAGONAL, *opposite,* updates a country kitchen short on storage and long on charm. In keeping with the scale of the open room and wainscoting, diamonds are 18 inches square on the diagonal. Noticeable grooves between the boards are part of the natural appeal of the distressed and aged look, which the owners emphasize with stools as plant stands. **See pages 156–159 for checkerboard technique.**

CHECKERBOARD, *right,* illustrates the color options for painted floors. Here, rather than opt for the classic black and white, the owners selected sage green and cream as an anchor for a kitchen and breakfast room designed around pink willowware and floral fabrics. The floor's pattern appears visually quieter than diamonds. **See pages 156–159 for checkerboard technique.**

GLAZED FADED FRESCO VARIATION, *left,* adds style to a budget remodeling, with a wall finish that gives character to a remodeled kitchen. As with faded fresco, the paint is brushed on in wide, loose, random strokes. However, for sheen, a finish coat of clear glaze was applied to the wall. **See pages 108–109 for faded fresco technique, and pages 128–129 for the smoked stain technique.** As a further economy move and style update, stock cabinets were stripped of glaze and color-washed with diluted latex paint**.** The repetition of the faded shades of green, from glazed walls to washed cabinets, upgrades the look of vinyl tile flooring and an economical laminate countertop. Black and white acts as a crisp, tailored accent. Keep in mind kitchens are ideal rooms for such improvements as they are typically seen as key selling points when a house is on the market.

SPONGED DIAMONDS, *left,* turn an ordinary wall into a harmonious backdrop for country-style furniture and collectibles. To achieve the look, the owners first painted the wall a rose color, then, after establishing a grid pattern, sponged over four coordinating, but visibly contrasting paint colors. Adding to the effectiveness of the technique are the carefully placed painted X's, created by not sponging the painted wall. Choose colors as a backdrop for your furnishings and consider repeating for a painted furniture piece. **See page 154 for technique.**

CHECKERBOARD FLOOR, *opposite,* animates a country kitchen of neutral colors and vintage furnishings. The fun comes from the 24-inch-square scale and the contrast with the narrow-striped walls. The taupe repeats for the window trim. **See pages 156–159 for checkerboard technique.**

HAND-PAINTED VINES, *right,* introduce a playful, more youthful mood into a small breakfast room with inherited furniture. The key to the success of this whimsical look is the oversize, stylized character of the hand-painted, curvy vines and white flowers. The edited palette of yellow, green, and white, based on the family's china, glassware, and collected pottery, works effectively with the lighthearted look. As a further unifying element, the vine's shade of yellow-green repeats for the base of the built-in and for the window trim. **See pages 148–149 for technique.** The wall behind the shelves contributes to the decorating scheme as decoratively painted as faux tiles, similar to a faux-tile technique on **pages 146–147.** To continue the visual interest, the floor is a crisp black-and-white checkerboard tile.

Liven up your library, home office, or den with a handsome decorative
finish you custom design to fit your style, skills, and room space.

kitchens **etc.**

PAINTED DIAMONDS, *opposite,* embellish a library by repeating, in paint, the tones of the wainscoting
and trim. The attention to color strengthens the tailored appeal and avoids the distraction of a competing color.
The lattice-like effect comes from the overlapping, darker paint. **See pages 130–131 for similar technique.**

PAINTED DIAMONDS, *above,* balance the carefully edited, two-color scheme of dark blue and brown
with white. The plaid upholstery fabric introduces an additional pattern for interest and warmth. The paint
treatment serves as a canvas for the nautical art and memorabilia. **See pages 130–131 for similar technique.**

RANDOM COMBING, *opposite,* dresses grayed taupe walls with a subtle hint of texture. For a den or office space, the technique imparts interest without the distraction of strong pattern and offers a low-key backdrop for books, collections, and art. In a home-office setting, choose the color and intensity that are comfortable for your work or study environment. Neutral base colors, such as grays, tans, and taupes, effectively showcase contemporary-style furnishings. **See pages 115 and 121 for combing techniques.**

PIN STRIPES, *above left,* derive their charm from a hand-painted interpretation of a classic look. To create, mark alternating 6- and 9-inch intervals along the top and bottom of a wall. Use a level and a straightedge to lightly pencil in vertical guides. (First center over a doorway or window and work outward.) Hand paint with metallic artist's paint from an art supply store. Pencil in the second line ¼-inch to the right of the first or simply paint it freehand.

RAGGING, *above right,* refreshes a small home office with the instant impact of color and texture. To avoid closing in a tight space, rag loosely in lighter colors and minimize contrast between values. Repeat the color in furnishings, such as this chair, to unify your scheme. In a room with a low, sloped ceiling, rag the ceiling for a flow of color that will make the room feel more open. **See pages 110–111; 128–129; and 150–151 for variations of ragging.**

STREAKY SQUARES, *opposite,* lend a note of sophistication and low-key texture to a study with a library feel. The oversize squares, which allude to cut and stacked stones, introduce an element of design interest without overwhelming framed art. The tailored look pairs handsomely with the mix of classic and contemporary furnishings often used for home offices. **See pages 132–133 for technique and page 64 for another room with this application.**

RAG ROLLING, *above,* warms a study with sleek furniture and contemporary art. For rooms where interest comes from the art, as here, choose closely matching paint colors that create a pleasing backdrop. When art is a major consideration, try paint techniques on larger pieces of scrap board to make sure the background you are creating will enhance your art. Tones reflect colors in the canvas and emphasize the graphic quality of contemporary hanging art pieces. **See pages 110–111 for technique.**

painttechniques

It's tempting to jump right in and start painting. Don't. You'll be happier with the results if you consider the size and scale of your room and your existing furnishings and patterns. **Begin by noting the ceiling heights, windows, and doors.** Then consider the size, placement, and patterns of your furniture. **Take everything into account before you decide on the scale of your painted pattern. Be particularly observant** when you are dealing with stripes, diamonds, or any of the repeated patterns. For example, wide stripes may fit the scale of a large room, but can overpower a child's tiny room. **For visually pleasing results,** take exact measurements of each of your walls. You'll need these measurements to calculate the dimensions of stripes and diamonds. **Whatever technique or techniques you choose, it is very important to practice** before you try a wall. If possible, work with a piece of drywall or smooth plywood 3- to 4-feet square to get a feel for a technique. **For the most successful project, keep the following painter-tested suggestions and tips in mind:**

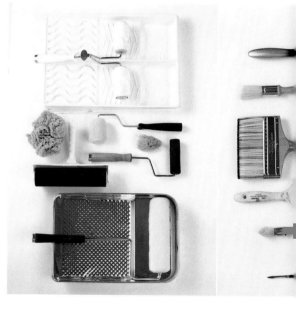

● **Plan your decorative painting projects** when you have several days to work on them. Individual steps need to be done quickly, but the overall processes take time. (For small rooms, you may only need several hours a day, but you may need two or three consecutive days to accomplish the necessary steps.) ● **Take the time to repair your walls if necessary.** And always tape smoothly and firmly, when necessary, for your project. ● **Try color combinations on a practice board.** In this book, many color combinations are within the same family. Using colors that are several shades from one another on the same paint chip card gives subtle and pleasing effects. ● **Read paint can labels to estimate paint.** Some cans of paint cover 300 square feet of painted wall, while some specialty paints cover only half that much. For glaze, you'll generally need only half as much as you would of regular paint. ● **Get help if you are painting more than small wall sections.** For example, one person can successfully paint below a chair rail, above a mantel, or a small powder room. Larger areas and more difficult projects are easier when done with a partner. ● **Choose the sheen of your base coat** according to your project and your skill level. The higher the sheen, the more decorative coats of paint or glaze will slide around, allowing for easier manipulation. If you use a flat base coat, it will act like a sponge and absorb color from top layers of paint. ● **Mix commercial glaze with paint or pigment** for transparent colors for walls. When using glaze, the more glaze added to the glaze/paint mixture, the more transparent the glaze will be. Commercially available paint conditioners, when used according to directions, can add a short amount of drying time to your glazes. ● **Use colored pencils that match your paint colors** to mark your walls. You may not have to erase the lines, and if you do, the marks are generally easier to remove

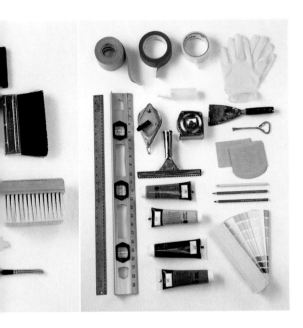

than those of regular lead pencils. If you have to use regular lead pencils, mark or draw as lightly as possible. ● **Keep a supply of drop cloths and clean rags at hand.** When using rags for application or removal of paint and glaze, be consistent with the kinds of rags used. An all-cotton rag will give a different effect than a blended or synthetic fiber. Other materials, such as crumpled newspapers or plastic bags, also vary the look. ● **Dampen your brush with water** before painting with the latex and water-based products used in this book. This helps keep paint from quickly accumulating and drying in the bristles and makes cleanup easier. ● **Consider the effects of humidity on your painting.** The water-based paints used in this book dry quickly. If your house has relatively high humidity, such as on a summer day, you will have more working time than on a dry winter day. You cannot stop in the middle of a wall when you begin a step. ● **Step back from the wall several times during each technique** to think about the wall as a whole and get a sense of composition. ● **Note that the skill levels** range from the least involved to the most involved. Skill level refers to the number of steps, measuring and taping, and difficulty. The time estimates are based on 9×12-foot rooms with 8-foot ceilings, but vary depending on size, ceiling height, weather, and familiarity with the technique. For best results, read the helpful hints for techniques.

● **TOOLS OF THE TRADE:** Select well-made brushes designed for your particular project. Depending on the job, you'll need everything from basic paint brushes to small artist's brushes to specialty-finish brushes. Add levels, straightedges, tapes, and combs to your supply list.

fadedfresco

LETTERED PHOTOS MATCH DIRECTIONAL STEPS

■ Tape off moldings, trim, and ceiling. Paint your walls with a satin-finish basecoat. (Light khaki was used here.) Water down flat white paint to a half-and-half mixture.

A With a 4-inch-wide brush, brush on the mixture with loose, random strokes. Vary your strokes so the mixture is more opaque in some areas, much lighter in others. Continue to brush out drips or runs, feathering the paint with your brush to avoid hard edges. Before the paint is completely dry, blend and wipe away some of the white with a clean, damp rag. Allow the walls to dry thoroughly.

B Make a color wash by mixing 4 tablespoons of burnt sienna into ½ gallon of water. Brush on liberally. As it dries, lightly brush runs to avoid drips. Be sure to cover the entire wall. (The paint will appear heavier in some areas.)

C After the walls are dry, repeat the color wash, using 4 tablespoons of yellow oxide to ½ gallon of water. Apply in the same manner as the previous color wash.

HELPFUL HINTS

■ This is a very messy technique. Applying color washes is like painting a giant watercolor on the wall. Be sure to have an ample supply of drop cloths and clean rags.

■ When mixing the paint and water, begin by adding a few tablespoons of water to the paint and mixing thoroughly. Add water slowly and continue to mix. If paint, especially acrylic paint, is added to a large amount of water all at once, it won't disperse. When mixing acrylic paints and water this way, stir the mix frequently to avoid pigments settling to the bottom. This mix cannot be stored because the pigments settle out.

■ Step back from the wall several times during each step and look to see where you might want to add or subtract a little color.

■ Be sure to work out to the edges of each wall, carefully getting paint into corners and all the way to the ceiling and down to the baseboards. This gives more unity to the walls.

■ Note that the finish will be fairly flat and not suitable for high-traffic areas. Attempting to wash it will remove pigment from walls. However, it can be clear-coated, but this affects the surface sheen. The technique works well on both smooth and textured walls.

SKILL LEVEL
Intermediate

TIME (NOT INCLUDING PAINTING BASE COAT)
1 day

SUPPLIES
■ Satin paint for base coat
■ Flat white wall paint
■ 4-ounce tube burnt sienna acrylic paint (from an art supply store)
■ 4-ounce tube yellow oxide acrylic paint
■ 4-inch brush
■ 3 buckets for mixing color washes
■ Drop cloths and clean rags
■ Blue painter's tape

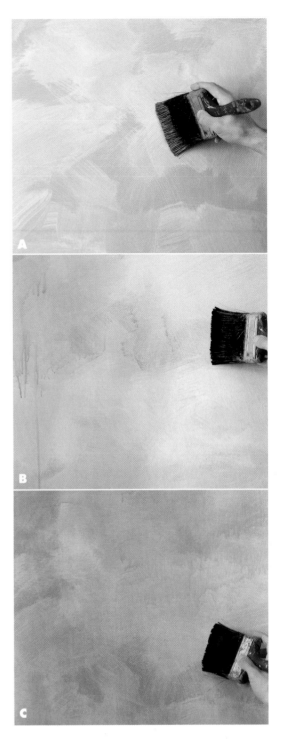

FADED FRESCO VARIATION
(PICTURED ON PAGES 10-12)

Follow the directions for faded fresco. However, instead of brushing on white, rag on white in two even layers over the entire painted wall (over red-based terra-cotta on pages 10–12). Allow to dry. Make two washes—from watered-down sienna and from watered-down yellow oxide acrylic. Brush on the sienna, then the oxide wash. (Artist acrylic paints are sold at art supply and crafts stores.)

rolling&ragging

LETTERED PHOTOS MATCH DIRECTIONAL STEPS

A **Tape off moldings, trim, and ceiling. Select two colors from the same family** that are near one another on a color chart. (Two shades of olive tans are used here.)

B **Pour each color into a separate paint tray.** Using small rollers, randomly roll each color on the wall.

C **Blend some as you go** so the wall is covered with variations of the two blended colors. Don't leave any hard lines. Allow the walls to dry thoroughly.

D **Choose a third color several shades lighter** than the lightest color used. Dilute the color with three parts water to one part paint. Wear gloves for protection. Submerge a cotton rag in diluted paint. Squeeze out paint. With the rag loosely wadded, press it against the wall. Try to have enough paint in the rag so it shows but not so much that it runs when pressing. Continue to turn the rag in your hand, re-gathering it and pressing it against the wall a dozen times or until you decide you need more paint. Continue this process over the entire wall.

■ **After the wall is dry,** rag on another layer of watered-down paint if you think too much of the under-painting is showing through.

HELPFUL HINTS

■ **This technique works well for smooth or textured walls.**

■ **The technique is very messy;** have lots of clean rags and drop cloths on hand.

■ **Half of a clean, cotton T-shirt,** with sleeves, neck, and hem removed, works well for this paint application.

SKILL LEVEL
Intermediate

TIME (NOT INCLUDING PAINTING BASE COAT)
1 day

SUPPLIES
■ Three flat paint colors within the same family on the color chart
■ Two paint rollers
■ Two paint trays and liners
■ Blue painter's tape
■ Bucket and stir stick for diluting paint
■ Drop cloths
■ Soft cotton rags
■ Latex or rubber gloves

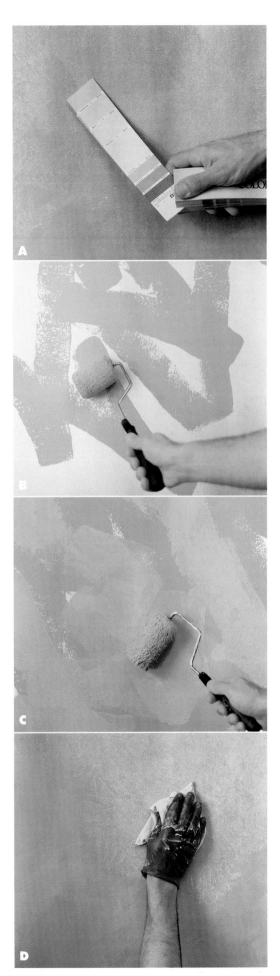

blendedspots

SKILL LEVEL
Beginner

TIME (NOT INCLUDING PAINTING BASE COAT OR SEALING)
1 day

SUPPLIES
- Semigloss paint for base coat paint
- 1 small tube black acrylic paint (from an art supply store)
- 1 small tube burnt umber acrylic paint (from an art supply store)
- Small artist's brush
- 4-inch, tapered, soft-bristle brush
- Paint palette
- Fine mist atomizer
- Water-based polyurethane
- Blue painter's tape

LETTERED PHOTOS MATCH DIRECTIONAL STEPS
- **Tape off moldings, trim, and ceiling. Paint walls with semigloss background color.** (White was used here.)

A Using the artist's brush, randomly dab small spots of black and burnt umber on the wall. Work in small sections about 2-feet-square.

B Dampen the 4-inch brush with water and in light sweeping motions, wipe across the paint spots to soften and blend against the background color. If paint spots dry too fast, moisten the wall with water from a fine mist spray atomizer. Continue this process across the wall, working one area into another.

- **To make this washable,** finish by coating the dry walls with a clear coat of glaze or water-based polyurethane.

HELPFUL HINT
- **The technique works best on smooth walls.**

moiré stripes

TIME (NOT INCLUDING
PAINTING BASE COAT)
Several days
(Measuring and taping
are time consuming.)

SUPPLIES

- Satin paint for
background color
- Glaze and paint
- 4-inch roller
- Small brush
- Paint tray and liner
- Bucket for glaze mix
- Level
- Tape measure
or ruler
- Colored pencil
- Rags
- Two-inch-wide blue
painter's tape
- Comb made from
7-inch squeegee
- Blue painter's tape

LETTERED PHOTOS MATCH DIRECTIONAL STEPS

- **Tape off moldings, trim, and ceiling. This
technique works best on smooth walls.**
- **Use satin paint for the background.** (A rich,
earthy yellow was used here.) Measure for the
placement of 5- to 6-inch stripes, making sure
that stripes are several inches away from the door
and window moldings and corners of the walls.
- **Using a level and a colored pencil** similar in
color to the paint, draw lines to determine the
width of stripes. Tape off floorboards and ceiling.
Tape off outside of stripes.
- **Mix the glaze mixture.** Start with half paint
and half glaze. (White paint with a dash of the
yellow base coat was mixed with the glaze for
the featured project.) Test the mixture on a
practice board for the appropriate color and
density. (The mixture should roll on easily without
dripping.) Adjust paint, color, or glaze as needed
to get the look you want. Using a small roller,
roll on the glaze mixture.

A **Immediately, using a comb made from a
squeegee,** and starting parallel to and against the
ceiling, make a continuous "S" pattern down the
length of the stripe. Be sure the comb covers the
width of the stripe without going beyond the outer
edges of the tape. Wipe paint from the comb.

B **Begin at the top again,** but this time, make
the reverse "S" pattern. This creates the moiré
stripes. Carefully remove the tape.

HELPFUL HINTS

C Make the squeegee comb by cutting out
grooves with a crafts knife.

- **It isn't important** that the stripes match
perfectly in width. Some can be a little wider
and others narrower.

linentechnique

SKILL LEVEL
Advanced

TIME (NOT INCLUDING PAINTING BASE COAT)
2 days

SUPPLIES
- Semigloss or gloss paint for base coat
- Acrylic textured glaze
- 6-inch weaver brush
- 2 lint-free, ¼-inch nap roller covers and frames
- Pencil or chalk line
- Edging tool
- Paint tray and liner
- Blue painter's tape
- General purpose masking tape
- Lint-free rags

LETTERED PHOTOS MATCH DIRECTIONAL STEPS

■ **Tape off moldings, trim, and ceiling. This is a two-person technique.** One partner should do all the "weaving" for a consistent look. As with all techniques, practice on a board first to make sure you are satisfied with the look. After you apply base coat to the wall, wait at least 24 hours to apply the decorative paint. The job takes at least two days as alternate panels are painted on alternate days.

■ **The project featured** here was created with the help of a kit that includes a video available at home centers and some specialty paint stores. (See page 160 for sources.) Because glaze dries quickly, it's best for panel widths not to exceed an easy arm's reach from standing or from a ladder, or approximately no wider than 42 inches. It's also important to carefully measure your room so that you can calculate the widths of the painted panels.

A **Use a pencil or chalk line to mark sections** at the top of the walls. Use a chalk line to snap lines down the wall. Snapping chalk lines is a two-person task. Tape just to the outside of chalk lines using blue painter's tape. Wipe chalk away, being careful to wipe away from the tape. Tape off the ceiling and trim.

■ **After taping, start with a section without windows or doors.** Expect to spend about 5 minutes on each section. To begin, pour the glaze into the roller tray and soak your roller for a minute. Roll to wipe off excess glaze. Working within the taped lines, roll a thin layer of glaze over the section. This project was done by rolling a V in the middle of the section and rolling out to fill. For best results, roll as close to the trim as you can reach and roll just over the seam tape. When you

finish rolling a section, roll back over lightly with light ceiling-to-floor strokes. The glaze will appear light and uneven. Dip the edging tool, included in the kit, into the glaze. With a pouncing motion, fill in hard-to-reach spaces around trim and in corners.

B **Using the weaver brush** and starting at the upper corner, drag from left to right. Use only the long side of the brush, not the tapered end. Wipe brush after each stroke. Reverse the motion over the first stroke. (Always start and stop on the tape.) Wipe off your brush. Continue down the length of the wall. Drag out from corners, rather than into corners.

C **To do the vertical "weaving,"** begin at the top of the wall and lightly move down with one stroke. Again, use only the long side of the brush. Do this very lightly so the horizontal lines are not erased. Wipe the brush and finish the wall section. Skip the adjacent section and begin the process again. Remove tape while the glaze is still wet. Allow the panels to completely dry for 24 hours.

D **Re-tape on top of the dried glaze.** Use general-purpose masking tape as painter's tape doesn't adhere to the glaze. Repeat paint technique until all sections are "woven."

HELPFUL HINTS

■ **This project was done with the help** of a kit, which includes an instructional video and tools. (See page 160 for sources.)

■ **For the prettiest look,** choose light colors, such as natural linen or pale pastels typical of summer linens.

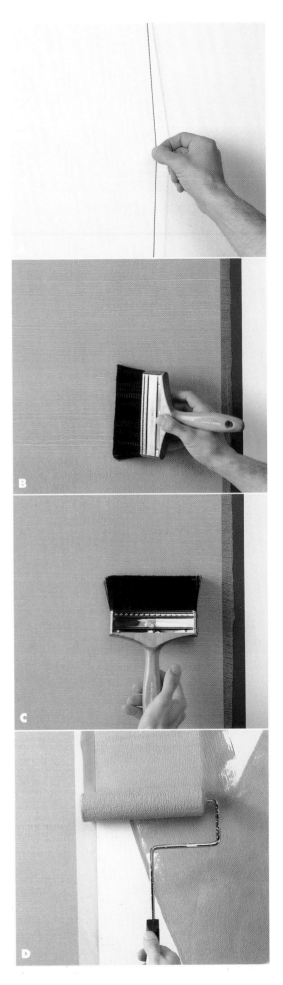

double-roll technique

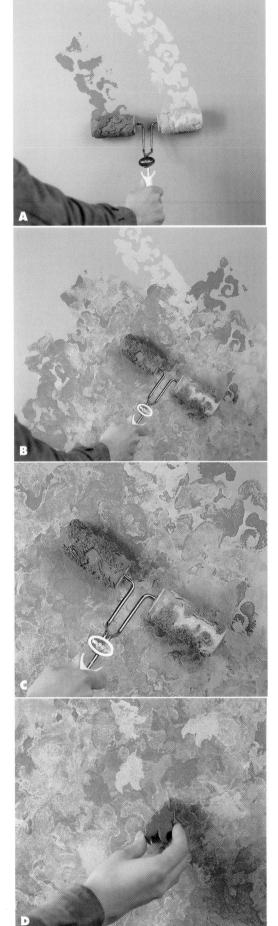

SKILL LEVEL

Beginner

TIME (NOT INCLUDING PAINTING BASE COAT)

1 afternoon for 1 wall

SUPPLIES

- Two coordinating colors of latex interior paint
- Double roller kit should include:
  - Double roller
  - Decorative roller covers
  - Double paint tray
  - Edging brush
  - Edging and accent sponges
  - Painter's masking tape

LETTERED PHOTOS MATCH DIRECTIONAL STEPS

- **Tape off moldings, trim, and ceiling. Start with painted walls in good condition.** This is your background color. Practice the following technique on a board to find the look you like. Pour paints into the divided paint tray. Don't mix paints. Dip a small "pouncing" or edging brush into both colors of paint. Using a dabbing motion, dab the paint into the corners and around the top edge of the wall. Starting at the top, paint only a small section of the edges and corners. It works best to do a two-foot section of edges and corners so they blend well into each other.

A&B Dip double roller into paints. Each side of the roller will be a different paint color. Roll with the double roller, up and down, and back and across until you get the amount of blending you like. Dip the accent sponge into paint and work the edges while they are still wet. It works best to do a wall in sections that you can roll easily.

C Continue rolling, edging, and accenting the wall. Take the time to step back and look at your work. Look for consistency. For variation, apply heavier pressure on one end of the roller and lighter on the other.

D For finishing touches, dip the accent sponge into the paint and press randomly. You can add additional accents, if you think they are necessary, after the wall is dry.

HELPFUL HINT

- **Double rolling is ideal for a focal point wall,** such as around the mantel, or in a small room such as a powder room. Select colors that blend, rather than contrast, for the most pleasing effect.

combing technique

Intermediate
(Complexity comes
from keeping lines
uniform.)

TIME (NOT INCLUDING
PAINTING BASE COAT)
2 days

SUPPLIES
- Satin, semigloss,
or gloss paint for base
coat
- Paint for topcoat
- 2-inch trim brush
- Small artist's brush
- 4-inch roller
- Paint tray and liner
- Rags
- Rubber comb
- Blue painter's tape

LETTERED PHOTO MATCHES DIRECTIONAL STEP

- **Tape off moldings, trim, and ceiling. Choose coordinating colors with enough contrast** to differentiate between the base and the combed top coat. (The base coat here is a grayed medium green, combed with a cream.) Paint the wall with a base coat. Allow the wall to dry thoroughly. Tape the trim. Use a roller to apply paint vertically to wall. Roll twice for approximately an 8-inch width.

A Holding the comb with both hands, apply even pressure and drag the comb down the wall in one continuous motion. Repeat the process, alternating between rolling and combing.

HELPFUL HINTS

- **This technique works well on smooth walls.**
- **If you are using a multisided rubber comb,** you may need to cut off one or two sides to allow the comb to reach into corners.
- **If the comb feels too flexible as you work,** tape it to a putty knife.
- **When you are using paint without glaze** as in this example, work only in small areas to avoid paint becoming unworkable. The addition of glaze will lengthen the drying time, but the technique is still most easily done in narrow sections.
- **When working from an inside corner to an outside corner,** begin at the inside. As you comb across the wall, you don't have to worry about the placement of the comb when you approach the outside corner.
- **When combing into an area narrower than the comb,** use a small brush and paint back slightly into the area already combed to widen the final width of paint to accommodate the width of the comb.

- **Comb adjacent walls on different days,** or if done in the same day, allow at least four hours between walls to avoid smudging.
- **Vary the look of basic combing** by combing zigzags, cross hatching, or swirls. You don't have to comb in a straight line.
- **This technique is fairly easy but requires a steady hand.** Corners can be tricky.

leathertechnique

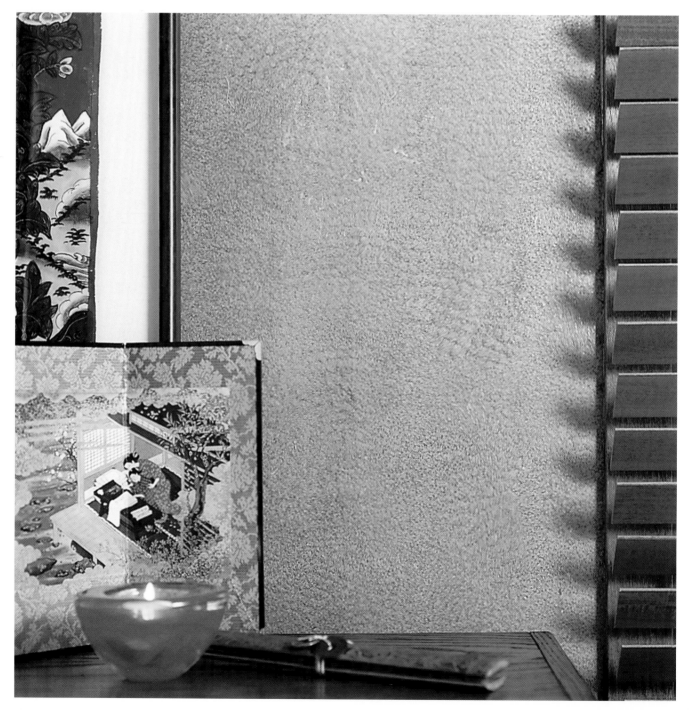

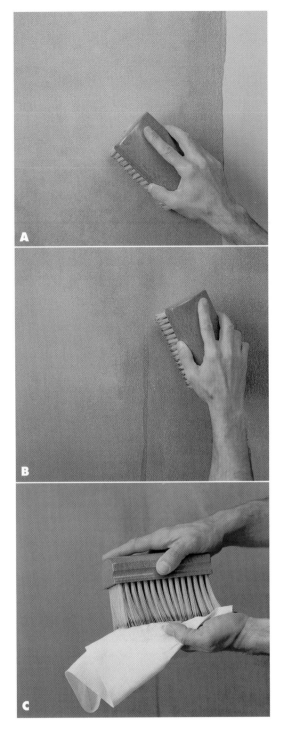

SKILL LEVEL

Advanced

TIME (NOT INCLUDING PAINTING BASE COAT)

2 days

SUPPLIES

- Semigloss or gloss paint
- Acrylic aging glaze
- Stippling brush
- Paint roller
- 2 lint-free, ⅜-inch roller covers
- Edging tool
- Blue painter's tape
- Paint tray and liner
- Lint-free rags

LETTERED PHOTOS MATCH DIRECTIONAL STEPS

- **Tape off moldings, trim, and ceiling. Paint the walls in your choice of color.** The rich colors of old leather furniture, such as browns, camels, aged gold, oxblood red, dark blue, or forest green, work well for this look. (The example here used an aged gold.) Allow the walls to dry overnight. As with all techniques, practice first on boards.
- **Make sure you have help;** creating leather walls takes two people. Tape off the ceiling, all trim, and adjacent walls. Pour the glaze into a paint tray; soak the roller in the glaze for a minute or so. Roll the roller back and forth so it doesn't drip. At the corner of the room, roll a single vertical stripe. Roll from the middle of this first section up toward the ceiling; roll down to evenly spread the glaze. Apply only a single strip of glaze.
- **Dip the edging tool into the glaze.** Dab glaze into hard-to-reach areas missed by the roller.
- **A Start stippling with your stippling brush** as soon as one strip of glaze has been rolled on. Brush in a quick, pouncing motion, beginning at the top of the wall and working down. Leave at least 2 inches of outer edge of strip not stippled.
- **B Roll another roller width of glaze** on the wall adjacent to the first, being careful not to overlap glaze of the first section. Quickly stipple to blend the seam between the two sections. Regularly alter the angle of your wrist when you stipple to avoid creating a pattern.
- **C Clean the bristles of your stippling brush** after every 15 or so pounces. Use the edging tool along the ceiling and molding to blend the stippled areas.
- **Remove the tape from the ceiling** and molding before the glaze is completely dry.

HELPFUL HINTS

- **Be prepared to work fast** as the glaze becomes unworkable in about 15 minutes. This is a fairly involved technique. For more detailed instructions, purchase a kit with an instructional video at a home center or specialty paint store.
- **If you can't complete a room in a day,** stop at a corner. Tape off the corner of the adjacent wall to make sure all the glaze stays on the side of the room you are completing.

chambray technique

SKILL LEVEL
Advanced

TIME (NOT INCLUDING
PAINTING BASE COAT)
2 days

SUPPLIES
- Semigloss or gloss paint
- Acrylic aging glaze
- 6-inch technique brush for chambray
- Paint roller
- 2 lint-free, ¼-inch nap roller covers
- Paint tray and liner
- Edging tool
- Pencil
- Chalk line
- Level
- Blue painter's tape
- Lint-free rags
- Masking tape

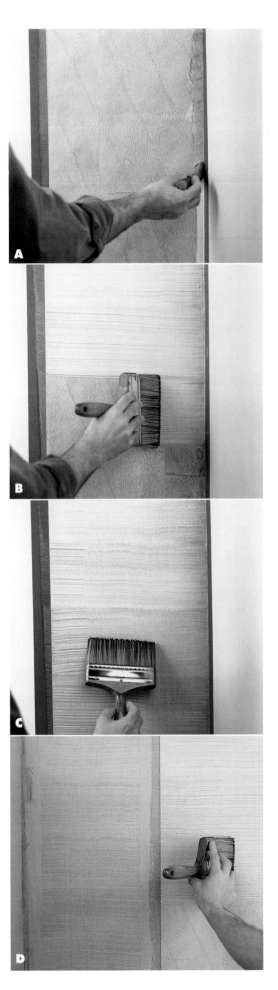

painter's tape.

- **Soak the roller in the glaze** and roll it over the tray so it doesn't drip. Roll a thin layer of translucent glaze within your taped panel. Roll as close to the ceiling and trim as possible. Even out roller marks by rolling from ceiling to floor. The glaze will appear uneven and translucent.

A **Dip the edging tool into the glaze.** With a pouncing motion, dab to corners in hard-to-reach areas, especially around trim and moldings. Apply just one layer.

B **Begin at the top of your panel and drag** the brush from one side to the other. Reverse the motion on top of the first stroke. Then repeat these two strokes for four horizontal drags; continue down the panel in this manner.

C **Begin at the ceiling and brush lightly** downward with one stroke. Don't bend the bristles. Repeat so each vertical line has been covered twice, leaving horizontal brush marks still visible. Remove tape. Allow to dry overnight.

D **Run masking tape down the dried glaze** about $\frac{1}{8}$ inch from the edge so only a very small area will be glazed twice. Complete the unglazed sections, using the same technique as the previously glazed panels.

HELPFUL HINTS

- **Light pastel shades,** which emulate open-weave fabrics, are attractive in this finish.
- **You must use the proper 6-inch weaver brush** for the desired effect. (See page 160 for sources.)

LETTERED PHOTOS MATCH DIRECTIONAL STEPS

- **Tape off moldings, trim, and ceiling. For best results with this technique,** purchase the appropriate kit with instructional video and tools from a home center or specialty paint store. (See page 160 for sources.) This is a two-person technique. However, for a consistent look, one partner should do all the weave painting. The other is the helper. The idea of chambray is to recreate the look of fabric panels with paint. Because glaze dries quickly, it's best for panel widths not to exceed easy arm's reach from standing or from a ladder, no wider than about 42 inches. It's also important to carefully measure your room so that you can calculate the widths of the panels. If you need to alter section widths to fit the space, place these sections at the corners. For example, depending on the size and configuration of your room, it may not be possible for every panel to be exactly your chosen 36 inches wide. If that is the case, do the adjustments at the corners of the room.
- **Use a pencil or chalk to mark sections at the top of the walls**. Use a chalk line to mark your lines. Wipe off the chalk after taping just outside the lines with blue

suedetechnique

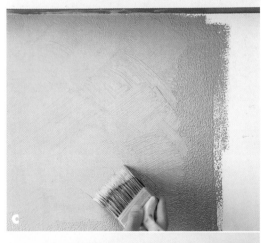

SKILL LEVEL

Advanced

TIME (NOT INCLUDING PAINTING BASE COAT)

2 days

SUPPLIES

- Specially-formulated textured paint
- Roller cover for textured paint and roller
- Guard for roller
- 3-inch brush
- Small sponge roller for cutting in
- Paint tray and liner
- Blue painter's tape

LETTERED PHOTOS MATCH DIRECTIONAL STEPS

■ **Tape off moldings, trim, and ceiling. Paints to create the textured effects of suede are sold under several brand names.** When you purchase the paint, it's important also to buy the roller covers formulated for your particular brand of textured paint. You'll use about twice as much textured paint to cover a room as you would for standard latex paint. For example, if you have painted a bedroom with one gallon of paint in the past, purchase two gallons of the textured paint. When correctly done, the finish is rich and handsome. However, it is difficult to touch up and is not resistant to moisture. It isn't recommended for kitchens, baths, children's rooms, or other high-traffic family areas. The projects for this book are in an adult sitting room and a master bedroom.

■ **Tape off all moldings**, trim, and ceiling.

A Cut in about two feet along the ceiling and down the corner of the wall. Use a small sponge roller.

B Using a large sponge roller, roll paint, two roller widths wide, in a vertical motion. Roll over wet paint from ceiling to floor.

C Brush into the wet paint with a cross-hatch motion, leaving a couple of inches unbrushed at the edge. Roll several more roller widths and continue to brush across wall in a cross-hatch motion from ceiling to floor. Allow to dry at least four hours.

D After paint has dried, dip brush in paint. Working quickly in small sections, cross-hatch a second coat of paint on the wall. It is important to work quickly so that you are always working into an edge of wet paint.

HELPFUL HINT

■ **One person should do** all cross-hatching so that the brush strokes are consistent.

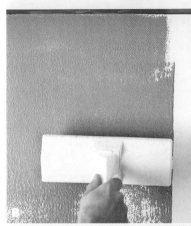

ragging off & smoked stain technique

SKILL LEVEL
Intermediate

TIME (NOT INCLUDING PAINTING BASE COAT)
2 days

RAGGING/SMOKED STAIN SUPPLIES
- Satin paint for base coat
- Acrylic artist's paint
- Glaze
- Bucket and stir stick to mix glaze
- Paint roller
- Paint tray and liner
- 4-inch trim brush
- Lint-free rags
- Drop cloth
- Blue painter's tape

After first applying glaze, make one continuous sweep with the brush as far as you can comfortably reach.

D Continue to lightly brush the glaze, feathering it out so it is darker in the corners and fades to lighter shades. (The idea is to re-create the look of a room aged by smoke.) On long stretches, continue the process along the length of the wall.

▪ **Glaze horizontal strokes one day and allow to dry overnight.** The next day, paint vertical strokes, making sure the glaze accumulates around moldings and in corners for the desired effect.

HELPFUL HINTS

▪ **This technique works well for smooth or textured walls.**

▪ **Commercially available paper rags work well.** They are sold in dispenser boxes and are sturdy and lint-free.

▪ **Note that fresh rags pick up more glaze** than saturated ones. Use accordingly as you work so you don't remove too much glaze every time you change rags.

▪ **You'll only have about ten minutes** to remove glaze before it becomes unworkable. Don't go back over a section that is partially dry. The glaze will not blend better.

▪ **For larger wall areas, enlist a partner.** One person should roll while the other blots with rags.

▪ **As an alternative to mixing your glaze,** use a commercially available one with pre-mixed pigments.

LETTERED PHOTOS MATCH DIRECTIONAL STEPS

▪ **Tape off moldings, trim, and ceiling. Paint the base coat with satin paint.** (A cream color was used here.) Add 4 tablespoons of acrylic artist's color to a quart of glaze. Stir well to mix. Cut in with the trim brush around the ceiling, baseboard, and corners as you go.

A Work in sections of about two roller widths at a time. Roll on two roller widths of glaze.

B With a clean, dry rag, blot the glaze so the rag removes some of the glaze. Continue blotting down the wall, replacing each saturated rag with a fresh one. Do not blot off to the edge of the wet glaze. It's important to roll down the next strip of glaze to the edge of the previously rolled portion of rolled glaze.

▪ **Begin ragging the seams to blend** the two sections. Then rag down the wall and continue the process across the wall.

▪ **Allow the ragged walls to dry thoroughly.**

SMOKED STAIN

C Mix the glaze as in ragging off.

▪ **Use the 4-inch trim brush to apply the glaze along the perimeter** of the walls and around window and door frames. Work in sections as wide as you can stretch your arms.

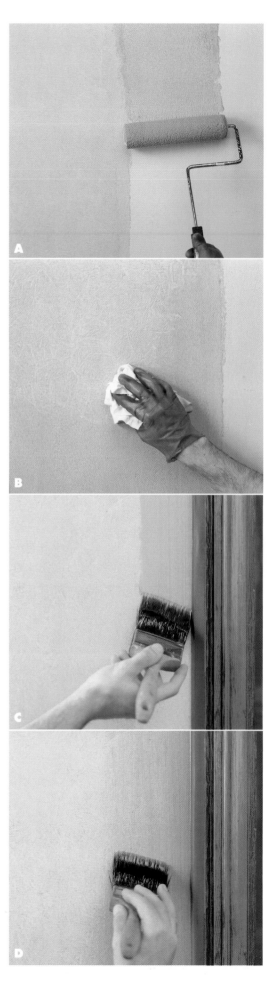

hand-painted diamond pattern

SKILL LEVEL
Intermediate

TIME (NOT INCLUDING PAINTING BASE COAT)
1½ to 2 days

SUPPLIES
- Paint in your choice of three colors
- Colored pencil and sharpener
- Cork-backed ruler
- Level with printed ruler
- Medium or large round, tapered artist's brush
- Small round, tapered artist's brush
- Quarter-size coin

every other mark will be 18 inches. You'll see a pattern emerging. When you finish measuring and marking, diagonally connect the lines with a colored pencil and ruler, and draw your grid.

A **To paint the diagonal grid**, use a medium or large round, tapered artist's brush dipped in your paint. Hand paint over the diagonal lines of the grid, starting at the top of one diagonal and moving all the way down to the bottom, dipping your brush as needed. Do all the diagonals in one direction first. If a second coat of paint is needed, simply dip your brush and trace over your lines again. Allow these lines to dry before you paint the other diagonals in the same manner.

B **After all of your lines are dry,** trace a quarter at each intersection. Using the smaller brush, paint in the circle.

C **After the circles are dry**, paint a ring around each circle with another color of paint, again using the smaller brush.

HELPFUL HINTS

■ **If you want a thicker or thinner line for the grid**, adjust your brush size accordingly. Adjust the size of the circle with a silver dollar or other circular object.

■ **Remember, the lines don't have to be perfectly straight.** The purpose of the hand-painted pattern is to add some interest and variety in line widths.

LETTERED PHOTOS MATCH DIRECTIONAL STEPS

■ **Choose the scale and placement** of the diamond pattern. In this project, the diamond is 18 inches in height and 15 inches in width. Finding the points of the diamond is the key to laying out the diamond grid.

■ **Begin by measuring and marking pencil dots** on the wall. Start at the corner where walls meet the ceiling and measure half of the width of your diamond design. Here, the full diamond width is 15 inches, so the measurement across is 7½ inches. Measure every 7½ inches across until you reach the end of the wall. Use your own measurements to best fit your space.

■ **After the horizontal measurements are in place**, measure down half the height of your diamond—here 9 inches. From the 9-inch mark, measure down 18 inches, then down another 18 inches, etc., until you reach the bottom of the wall.

■ **Return to the top of the wall** and locate your first half-width mark. Measure down from there to 18 inches, again using your level, and every 18 inches until you reach the bottom. Continue measuring down the wall in this manner. Remember that the first mark down will be 9 inches from every other mark at the top of the wall. And

streakysquares technique

SKILL LEVEL
Intermediate

TIME (NOT INCLUDING PAINTING BASE COAT)
2 days

SUPPLIES
- Paint for base coat
- Three colors of paint for streaks
- 2-inch paint brush
- Colored pencil
- Level with printed ruler
- Blue painter's tape

LETTERED PHOTOS MATCH DIRECTIONAL STEPS

■ **Tape off moldings, trim, and ceiling. Choose the scale for your room.** Measure the walls to determine what dimensions will work. If your measurements won't come out evenly, fudge a bit at the corners of your walls where exact measurements aren't as obvious. Twenty-four-inch squares were chosen for this project. Paint the background color. Allow to dry.

■ **Make a grid on your wall by marking off** every 24 inches on your wall. Start at the top corner. Mark every 24 inches across the top of the wall and down the corner to the floor. Extend the marks from the ceiling down to the floor, using a level and pencil. Next, extend the horizontal marks out from the corner in the same manner.

■ **Now you have a simple grid.** Squares should alternate between horizontal and vertical streaks. To keep the horizontal and vertical patterns in the correct order, mark either a horizontal or vertical arrow in each square with your colored pencil.

A **Mask off every other square** in the uppermost horizontal lines of squares. Work one square at a time. Open your three small cans of paint. You need to work quickly within each square. Dip your brush into the lightest color and streak the square. Gradually streak in the medium shade. Be careful not to apply too much paint to avoid drips.

B&C **Add the darkest paint for accents.** Work each square until you achieve the look you want, but do so quickly enough that the paint doesn't dry between steps.

■ **Carefully remove the tape from each finished square.** When you tape off the square between the finished squares, keep in mind that you may allow a little bit of the background color to show through by not butting the tape directly up to the adjacent finished square. The background color showing through provides contrast to the streaks.

■ **Repeat the taping and streaking** until all the squares are completed.

HELPFUL HINT

■ **Choose three colors varying in value and intensity** from a paint chip card. Paint stores often have five to six tones of one color on a paint chip card. Choose a light, medium, and dark accent color. To choose a background color, think of a color that will provide a touch of contrast. For example, the background color here is a cool gray, which contrasts with the warm golden brown tones of the streaky squares. Do not make the background color too bright; only a little contrast is necessary.

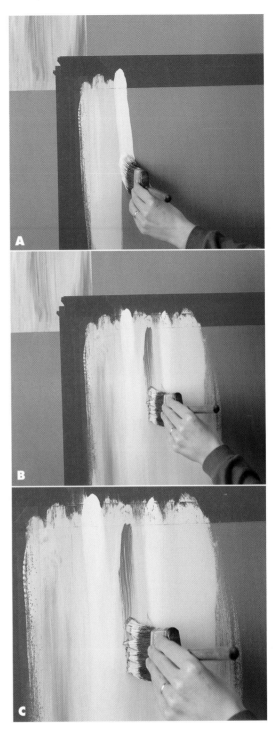

hand-painted vertical stripes

SKILL LEVEL

Beginner

TIME (NOT INCLUDING PAINTING BASE COAT)

1 day

SUPPLIES

- Paint for base coat
- Paint for stripes
- Level with a printed ruler
- 2- or 3-inch paint brush
- Colored pencil
- Blue painter's tape

LETTERED PHOTOS MATCH DIRECTIONAL STEPS

■ **Tape off moldings, trim, and ceiling. Choose your colors and widths.** The colors may contrast or be differing values of the same color.

■ **Start at the top of the wall** and make a series of measurement marks moving horizontally across the top. In this project, the stripes are 6 inches wide with 4 inches between each. If you want to avoid a stripe around a corner, it's acceptable to fudge your measurements a bit. Or you can allow the stripe to fold around the corner, depending on your preference.

A & B When the measurements are completed, use a level to draw lines from ceiling to floor. Draw lines lightly and use a colored pencil if possible. Protect the moldings and trim with painter's masking tape.

C For a charming, hand-painted look, simply paint the stripes on the wall, starting at the edges and filling in. It works best to start at the top and paint in about 12-inch sections. If necessary, apply a second coat after the first is thoroughly dry. Carefully remove painter's tape while paint is still wet.

strié (dragging) technique

SKILL LEVEL

Intermediate

TIME (NOT INCLUDING PAINTING BASE COAT)

1 day

SUPPLIES

- Satin paint in your color choice
- Tinted glaze
- Large, stiff-bristled brush
- Roller
- Blue painter's tape
- Rags

LETTERED PHOTOS MATCH DIRECTIONAL STEPS

- **Tape off moldings, trim, and ceiling. This technique requires two people.** Make sure your walls are smooth. Choose a background color which will show through the glaze.

A The basic technique is rolling glaze over the painted wall and then removing some of the glaze by dragging a brush with stiff bristles from the top to the bottom of your walls.

B This allows some of the background color to show through and creates a pleasing visual texture.

- **One partner rolls the glaze in vertical stripes**; the second removes some of the glaze by dragging the brush down the wall. Bristles need to be lightly touching the wall for best effect. Maintain a light, steady pressure.
- **Wipe the dragging brush on clean rags** to prevent it from being overloaded.

HELPFUL HINTS

- **One partner should be rolling the second vertical stripe while the other partner is finishing dragging the first.** Stripes should overlap.
- **Both partners should work quickly**; neither can stop in mid-wall. Tape off adjacent walls so glaze doesn't seep around corners.
- **If you find it difficult to drag down in one continuous motion,** stop two-thirds of the way down the wall and drag from the bottom up, feathering your brush up as the lines meet. Stagger the meeting points to avoid the distraction of a horizontal band appearing around the lower portion of your wall.

sponging technique

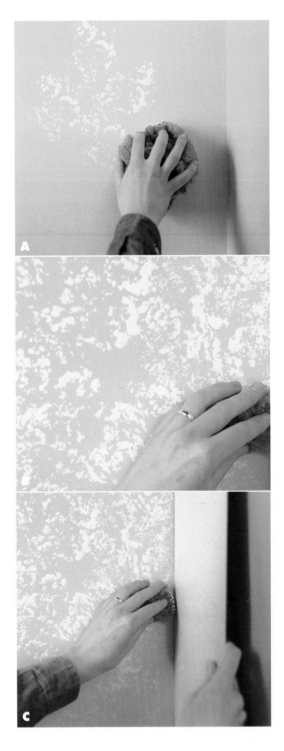

SKILL LEVEL

Beginner

TIME (NOT INCLUDING PAINTING BASE COAT)

½ to 1 day

SUPPLIES

- Paint for base coat
- Paint for sponging
- Natural sea sponge
- Paint tray and liner
- Newspapers for blotting
- Cardboard for corners

LETTERED PHOTOS MATCH DIRECTIONAL STEPS

■ **For this project, diluted off-white paint was sponged over pale yellow walls.** If you are painting a base coat, allow it to dry overnight.

A **Wet your sponge with water**, wringing it out thoroughly. Pour a small amount of paint into a tray or pie tin. Dip the sponge into the paint and blot excess on newspaper. Cup the sponge in your hand and push lightly onto the surface.

B **Space the patches of color evenly**, but change the position of the sponge for an irregular, mottled effect. Close, overlapping marks have a sleek look; widely spaced sponging with little or no overlapping appears more casual. Try spaced first; then fill in.

C **Use a piece of cardboard**, held up with one hand in a corner, to protect the opposite corner from being over-sponged. Use a small piece of sponge to work in corners.

HELPFUL HINTS

■ **For the most pleasing effect**, choose colors without jarring contrast. If you want to add second and third layers, consider choosing your colors from the same paint card for a pleasing, subtle effect.

■ **As an alternative**, loosely rag on diluted paint with a lightly gathered, not rolled, cotton cloth. Blend as you rag for a pleasing effect.

color wash & taped stripe technique

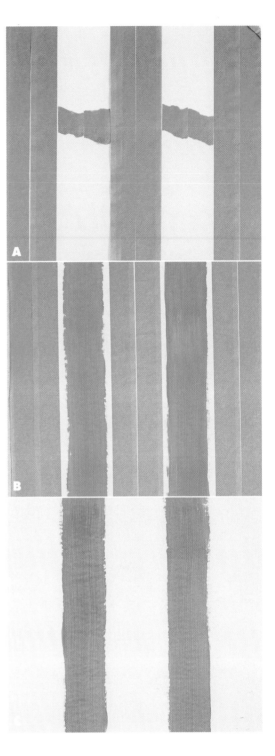

SKILL LEVEL

Beginner

TIME (NOT INCLUDING PAINTING BASE COAT)

1 day

SUPPLIES

- Paint for base coat
- Paint for stripes
- Latex glaze
- Pencil
- Level
- Brown paper painter's tape in desired width
- 3- to 4-inch paint brush

LETTERED PHOTOS MATCH DIRECTIONAL STEPS

- **Tape off moldings, trim, and ceiling. The purpose of taped stripes is to simplify measuring.** The glaze, which is brushed on, contributes hand-painted charm. You'll use the width of two pieces of tape, as shown, as the spacing between your stripes. The width of your brush is the width of your stripes.

A Tape the spaces between stripes; this will be the unpainted part of the wall. Using the painter's tape, tape two pieces together down the wall. Next, use two smaller pieces of the same tape for spacing. Repeat two pieces of tape, running down the wall as shown. Repeat this pattern across the wall. Fudge measurements slightly at corners to compensate for spacing. If you are concerned that taped lines are straight, first create a guideline with a pencil and level.

B Mix a glaze mixture from 1 part paint, 1 part latex glaze, and 1 part water. Adjust proportions if the mixture seems too thick or too thin. Remove the pieces of spacer tape. Using a brush slightly narrower than the stripes, drag down the glaze mixture from the ceiling.

C Remove the tape while the glaze is still damp.

flowerborder technique

SKILL LEVEL

Beginner

TIME (NOT INCLUDING PAINTING BASE COAT)

½ to 1 day

SUPPLIES

- Three colors of latex paint
- Small paint brush
- Artist's brushes
- Level with printed ruler
- Colored pencil

LETTERED PHOTOS MATCH DIRECTIONAL STEPS

- **The fun of this border is its lighthearted,** stylized look. Choose bright, clear colors for an appealing effect.

A Measure with level and pencil in two horizontal lines at the desired height. Here, the lines are 8 inches apart. Measure and lightly mark center points every 9 inches.

B With a small brush and the border paint color, draw an outline of the daisy around every other spot. Draw a small circle around the other spots.

C Paint the border with your color choice.

D Paint the flowers' center in the second color and the spots in the border with a third color.

HELPFUL HINTS

- **Standard chair rail** height is 32 to 34 inches.
- **Note the pencil lines,** which are marked heavily to be visible for instruction. For your home projects, mark as lightly as possible to avoid dark lines showing through.

sponge-stamped brick pattern

STAMPED BRICK
SKILL LEVEL
(PHOTOGRAPH A)
Beginner

TIME (NOT INCLUDING PAINTING BASE COAT)
2 days

SUPPLIES
- Satin paint for base coat and sponging
- Paint tray or shallow container
- Additional tray or shallow container to blot sponge
- Kitchen sponge

PATCHWORK QUILT
SKILL LEVEL
(PHOTOGRAPH B)
Intermediate

TIME (INCLUDING PAINTING BASE COAT)
2 days

SUPPLIES
- Paint for base coat
- Four 2-ounce jars acrylic artist's paint
- Boat-and-deck sponge
- Level
- Plastic plate
- Serrated knife
- Pencil

STAMPED BRICK (PHOTOGRAPH A)

■ **Tape off moldings, trim, and ceiling. Paint the base coat.** Choose a coordinating color for the sponge stamping. Remove the kitchen sponge from its wrapper. Mark an arrow on one broad side of the sponge. This indicates the orientation to use the sponge. By placing the sponge on the wall the same way each time, the sponging sets up a pattern on the wall.

■ **Pour a small amount of paint into a shallow container.** Hold the sponge by the marked side and lightly dip the reverse side into the paint. Blot the sponge on the second container to remove excess paint. There should be enough paint on the sponge to stamp it four or five times.

A **When you are confident in your technique,** carefully place the dipped and blotted sponge against the wall. Apply even pressure over the surface of the sponge with the palm of your hand.

■ **Carefully peel back the sponge, carefully realign, and repeat the process.** The sponge print should be crisp and clear. There will be some variation, sometimes lighter or darker.

■ **Occasionally, step back and look at the wall** to intentionally use the variation for interest. Start at the top of a wall in the corner, stamping a line across the wall against the ceiling.

■ **When you come to the next corner,** the sponge may not match up perfectly with the corner. Leave this for now. (Later when the room is almost complete, you can cut the sponge to a size that fills any gaps.)

■ **Stamp the second row.** Continue this process, working down the wall and being careful to align the sponge. Keep the row straight across the wall.

PATCHWORK QUILT (PHOTOGRAPH B)

■ **Tape off moldings, trim, and ceiling.** The stamped quilt grid is planned for a 6- x 8-foot wall or can be painted as a quilt on a larger wall. Each block of the quilt square is 6 stamps by 6 stamps, which is about 25½ inches square. For best results, measure your wall and make a graph before you start.

■ **Wash the new sponge in soap and water,** and allow to dry into a firm block. With a serrated knife, cut the sponge to a 2⅝-inch square.

■ **Place a few tablespoons** of your first color into the plate and lightly dampen the sponge. Practice on paper first to get the stamped look you like. When the base coat is dry, mark a vertical line 2¼ inches from the corner of the wall if you want the design to begin at a corner. At the top of the vertical line, place one tip of the stamp. Place the opposite tip below it on the line and press. Continue stamping down the line.

B **Count down six stamps from the top.** At the center tip of the sixth stamp, draw a horizontal line across the wall with the level. Count down another six stamps and mark another horizontal line. Continue drawing horizontal lines until you reach the bottom of the wall. Stamp with the same paint, refilling as needed.

■ **On one of the horizontal lines of stamps,** count six stamps to the right of the first vertical line. At the center tip of this stamp, mark a vertical line from the top to the bottom of the wall with the level. Count another six stamps to the right and mark another vertical line. Continue drawing vertical lines until you reach the corner. Stamp the vertical lines with the same paint as above to establish the grid pattern.

■ **Start over with your next paint color.** Inside each square, stamp the next color. When this is completed, stamp the third color. Complete with the fourth. Leave the last five blocks of the wall's base coat unstamped.

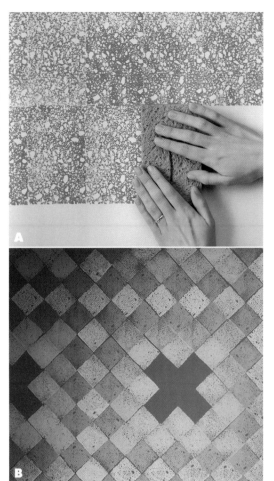

faux tile floor technique

FAUX-TILE FLOOR
SKILL LEVEL
Intermediate

TIME (NOT INCLUDING
PAINTING BASE COAT)
1 day

SUPPLIES
- Primer
- Latex or porch paint
- 1- or 2-inch flat
artist's brushes
- No. 7 artist's brush
- Three coordinating
colors of latex paint
- Two colors of
crafts paint
- Polyurethane
- Paint trays and liners
- Colored pencil
- Straightedge

LETTERED PHOTOS MATCH DIRECTIONAL STEPS

■ Tape off baseboard molding. This pattern was created by drawing a grid of squares in a diagonal pattern across the floor. For best results, use graph paper to draw to scale the perimeter of the floor and the grid pattern so you can see how the pattern lays on the floor. Prime the floor with latex primer following manufacturer's instructions.

A Using a pencil, very lightly draw a straight line from one corner of a square to the opposite corner, bisecting the square and leaving it divided into two triangles. Continue these lines across the floor so half the squares are bisected and half of the squares are whole.

B With a 1- to 2-inch flat artist's brush, loosely fill in the squares with your choice of latex paint. Leave about ⅜-inch of white around the perimeter of each square. Fill in the triangles with two other latex colors, in the same loose manner, again leaving some white around the perimeter of each.

C Use a damp rag to wipe off pencil lines.

D With a No. 7 rounded artist's brush, paint freehand circles with crafts paint at the intersections where six points of squares and triangles meet. With the same brush and the second color of crafts paint, paint dashed lines through all of the white areas that surround the squares and triangles.

■ Seal with two coats of water-based, satin-finish polyurethane, allowing adequate drying time between the coats.

FAUX-TILE WALL (PICTURED ON PAGE 83)

■ Start with a light, clean wall; paint off-white if necessary.

■ If the wall is freshly painted, allow it to dry thoroughly. Using a straightedge, level, white paint, and small brush, freehand paint the mortar lines that will divide 4x4-inch tiles. Paint the mortar lines freehand—don't tape— to keep the effect loose and casual. For easy spacing, start at the center of each wall and work out.

■ Using a small roller for each color, paint inside mortar lines. While the paint is wet, brush over each tile; use separate brushes for each color.

■ Allow the painted wall to dry thoroughly. Thin leftover off-white paint with acrylic urethane and brush over the walls for a color-washed effect.

FAUX-TILE WALL

SKILL LEVEL
(PICTURED ON PAGE 83)
Intermediate

TIME (NOT INCLUDING PAINTING BASE COAT)
1 day

SUPPLIES
■ Eggshell finish, off-white latex paint
■ Eggshell finish, white latex paint (quart)
■ Two shades of latex paint in your colors
■ Paint tray and liner
■ Two small rollers
■ Small paint brushes
■ Acrylic urethane
■ Straightedge and level
■ Brown masking tape

hand-painted vine pattern

SKILL LEVEL
Beginner

TIME (NOT INCLUDING PAINTING BASE COAT)
1 day

SUPPLIES
- Paint for base coat
- Green crafts paint for vines and leaves
- Crafts paint for accent color
- Pencil
- Level with printed ruler
- Small tapered artist's brushes

LETTERED PHOTOS MATCH DIRECTIONAL STEPS
- **Measure your walls.** Determine the number and spacing of the vines you would like.

A Measure and mark pencil spots so they line up equal distance both vertically and horizontally.

B Connect the spots vertically with alternating curving lines.

C With an artist's brush, paint the vertical lines.

D Paint leaves using the inside curve of each vine as a guide. Add round accents in a third color below each leaf, or randomly as shown in *opposite* photograph.

HELPFUL HINTS
- **Use colored pencils if possible.**
- **Choose** a round, tapered No. 10 artist's brush to hand paint vines and leaves.
- **Practice your leaf technique on a board** before you attempt the wall.

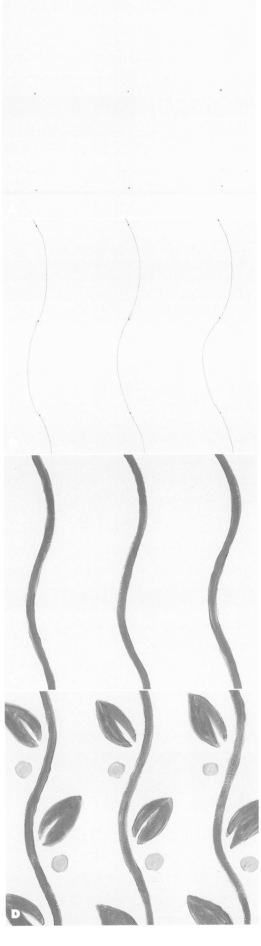

large-scalediamond pattern

SKILL LEVEL
Intermediate

TIME (NOT INCLUDING PAINTING BASE COAT)
1 day

DIAMOND SUPPLIES
- Satin paint for base coat
- Glaze
- Paint to tint glaze
- Colored pencil
- Ruler
- Level with printed ruler
- Rags
- Small paint roller or brush
- Paint tray and liner
- Blue painter's tape

BASIC RAG ROLLING SUPPLIES
- Semigloss latex paint for background
- Paint or glaze for ragging
- Roller or brush
- Paint tray and liner
- Clean rags

LETTERED PHOTOS MATCH DIRECTIONAL STEPS

■ **Determine the size, color, and location of the diamonds.** Base your decision on the size of your room and the size, location, and color of your furniture and fabric patterns.

■ **After you determine pleasing dimensions** for your diamonds (20 inches wide x 30 inches high here), measure from the bottom of your wall up to find the bottom tip of your first diamond. If you are going to wrap your design around a corner to cover two walls, start your first diamond in the middle of the corner, half of the diamond on one wall and half on the other.

A Use a level with a ruler to measure, to find the top point of the diamond. (Here it is 30 inches.) Find the middle of the diamond—here 15 inches. Find the horizontal right and left points of the diamond by measuring 10 inches to the right and left, keeping these points level with the middle point.

■ **Repeat until all diamonds are drawn.** The other diamonds are easier to measure as you have already established the bottom, top, and middle points. Use your level from these points to establish the points of the next diamond. Tape off every other diamond just outside the penciled lines.

B Mix one part glaze to one part

paint. Add more glaze if it appears too thick. Roll the glaze over one diamond at a time.

C Rag off with a damp, clean rag. This removes some of the glaze for a textured look.

D Wait for about a minute, then rag off a little more glaze. Work with the glaze until the resulting look appeals to you.

■ **Try to work all the diamonds in a similar fashion**, but remember that each one should and will be a little different from the next. Remove the tape from the glazed diamonds after the first set of diamonds has dried. Then tape and glaze remaining diamonds.

BASIC RAG ROLLING
(EXAMPLES INCLUDE PICTURES ON PAGES 74 AND 75.)

■ **This works best as a two-person job.** Practice first on scrap board to achieve the desired look. The effect varies with the rag fabric. Choose natural fibers, such as cotton sheets or T-shirts, that hold paint.

■ **Prepare the fabric by twisting strips** into tight, 6-inch-long, sausage-like rolls. Prepare enough rolls to do an entire wall or room. A 12×14-foot room may need as many rags as the equivalent of a double-bed sheet.

■ **Apply a base coat of semigloss paint** or tinted glaze; allow it to dry completely.

■ **Apply a second coat** of a coordinating color, using a roller or brush. Make sure the background color is several values lighter than the paint you apply on top.

■ **While the second coat is wet,** roll the rag lightly over the surface from top to bottom, holding it at both ends. This exposes the base coat.

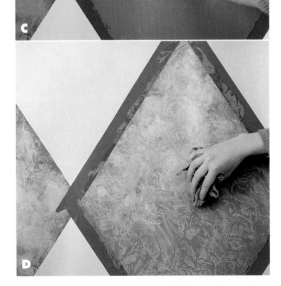

plaidtechnique

SKILL LEVEL
Advanced

TIME (NOT INCLUDING PAINTING BASE COAT)
2 to 2½ days

SUPPLIES
- Four colors of satin paint
- Level with printed ruler
- Colored pencils to match your paint colors
- Rectangular kitchen sponges
- Paint trays and liners
- Rags
- Paper bag for blotting
- Blue painter's tape
- Sharp scissors

LETTERED PHOTOS MATCH DIRECTIONAL STEPS

■ **For the best results**, decide on the colors and scale of your plaid and practice on boards until you perfect a pattern you like. (For this project, tan, green, and light blue paint were used.) Layer your color choices in different combinations and try small, medium, or large kitchen sponges to change your scale. You may like a simpler plaid design with one or two colors and a less complex pattern.

■ **To create your pattern**, you'll measure out the largest part of the plaid, which is the background plaid that is sponged on by the whole, flat sponge. The other two plaid colors are sponged on with the sides of the sponge. These thinner bands are applied over the dried thicker plaid. Tape off moldings, trim, and ceiling.

■ **Start the plaid in the most prominent area** of the wall. Refer to the graphic pattern for measuring on **page 154**. The sponge used in this example was 3½ inches wide on the broad side and 1-inch wide on the edges. These two measurements from the sponge create the layout.

■ **Referring to the graph on page 154**, measure and mark the vertical lines of the largest part of the plaid. Use a level to extend from your mark to make the vertical lines run from the top of the wall to the bottom.

■ **Lay in the horizontal lines of the large plaid**. Measure the same distance as before, but horizontally only. Use the level to extend the horizontal lines all the way across your wall. This is the basic structure of your plaid.

■ **Wet the sponge and wring it out**. Pour a small amount of paint into the paint tray and gently dip your sponge into the paint, then immediately blot off excess paint on the clean end of the

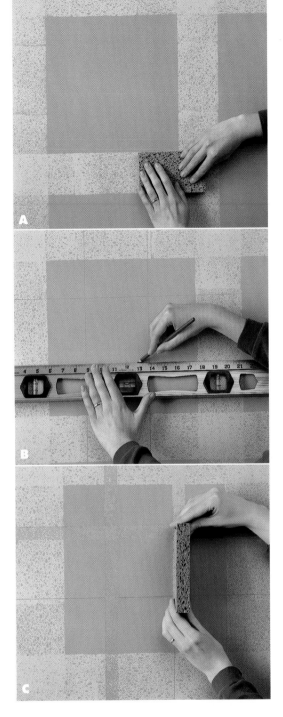

paint tray and/or on a paper bag.

A **Begin sponging the vertical lines.** Keep the sponge to the right of the vertical line and press firmly with the sponge placed vertically on the wall. You will be able to sponge three to four times before you have to dip into the paint. An arrow drawn on the back will help to orient the sponge in the same direction each time.

■ **Continue sponging until all the verticals** are in place. If you have a tight spot where the sponge is too large to fit, wait until you are done with most of the room and cut down the sponge to fit. If the plaid doesn't break evenly at a corner, wait until the end and cut down the sponge to fit.

Sponge horizontal lines by placing the sponge on the under side of penciled-in horizontal lines.

B **After the largest part of the plaid dries**, draw the vertical and horizontal lines for the smaller parts of the plaid, on top of the existing plaid. Refer to the second graph on **page 155** for help with measurements and layout. Sponge in the thin parts of the plaid. Starting and finishing with the second color, before you start the third color.

C **Use the narrow edges of your sponge** and sponge to the right of the penciled lines. Trim down the sponge if necessary to fit into tight spaces. A second or third sponge may be used to trim down if necessary.

1

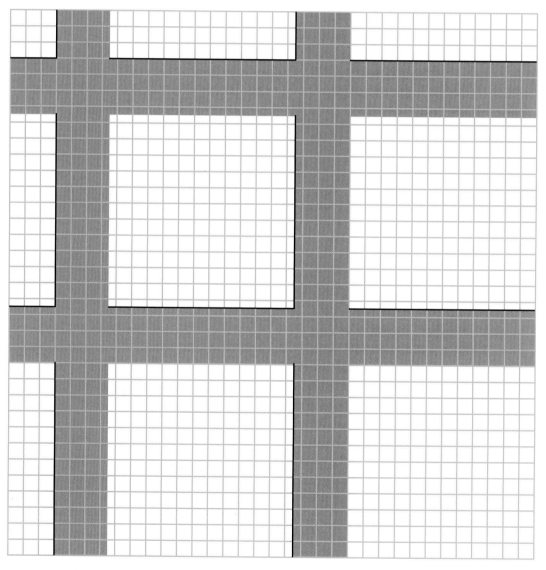

1 SQUARE = 1 INCH

HELPFUL HINTS

■ **This is a good technique to repeat** wall colors used in your home.

■ **Because the technique is time consuming**, consider it for small rooms or as a focal point.

■ **Windowless walls are easiest** as they are uninterrupted. (Here the plaid was used in a windowless bath; **see page 33.**)

2

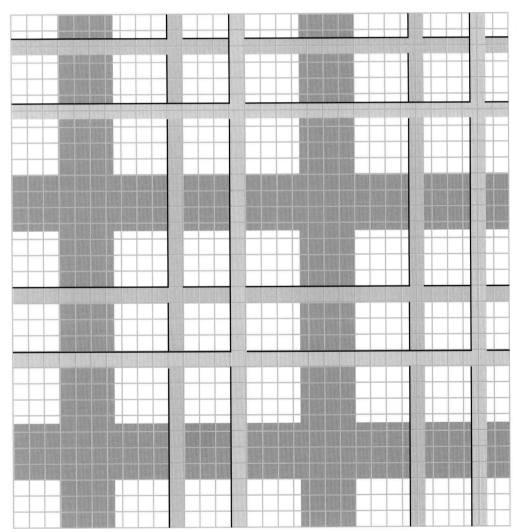

1 SQUARE = 1 INCH

checkerboard floor technique

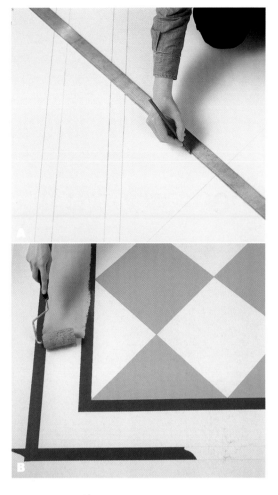

SKILL LEVEL
Advanced

TIME (NOT INCLUDING PAINTING BASE COAT)
1 to ½ days

SUPPLIES
- Two paint colors (porch paint recommended for durability)
- Small touch-up brushes
- 4-inch roller cover and frame
- Paint trays and liners
- Ruler
- Yardsticks
- Chalk line
- T-square or right triangle
- Masking tape
- Polyurethane

LETTERED PHOTOS MATCH DIRECTIONAL STEPS

- **Decide on the placement of your checkerboard floor design** and whether a border will be included. Any size of "area rug" can be painted onto a wood or concrete floor, or the floor can be filled as in the example, *opposite* . The checkerboard could also be placed on a diagonal.

- **Prepare your floor by scraping loose paint**, sanding, and wiping up any dust. The surface should be clean and smooth. Seal your surface with an appropriate primer if it isn't already sealed and follow directions on the can of porch paint.

- **If you are putting the checkerboard design** in the middle of a room or at an angle, decide on the size of the rug. If you are adding the border, lay out the basic rectangle that will be the outside border. For best results, carefully measure your floor area. Then design your checkerboard pattern on graph paper so you know exactly what measurements to use. Or, if you are including a border, you can lay out the border on all sides, then measure and divide the remaining space to find the size of the checkerboard.

- **Make two points to establish one side of the rectangle.** Connect the lines with a yardstick. If working with a partner, which is helpful, you can snap a chalk line. Or use two or three yardsticks taped together to make a long straightedge if you are working alone.

- **Use a right triangle or a T-square** to square the edges for the next side of the rectangle.

- **Extend your yardstick(s) or chalk line** to line up with the right angle you made with the T-square or right triangle. Mark your line with the chalk or pencil.

■ **Repeat this procedure for the third side**, then simply connect the edges for the fourth side. Tape off this rectangle and paint it your lightest color.

■ **Measure from the outside edge** of the rectangle to the inside to create the borders. Draw in the borders, using the ruler for measuring, the right angle for 90-degree angles, and the yardsticks for a straight edge. See diagram *below*.

■ **The diamond checkerboard pattern** is based on a grid. Measure the shorter side inside the borders and divide by three or more, depending on how many diamonds you want to go across your checkerboard pattern. Measure and divide the long side by five or more, again depending on your space and taste.

A **Mark all of the measurements** into the inside border. Connect the marks diagonally to make the checkerboard design. Or mark the other points of the diamond checkerboard pattern, by using the measurements you figured out on graph paper. This technique is easier if you have to work alone. You can connect all of your marks diagonally, sliding your straightedge as you go.

1

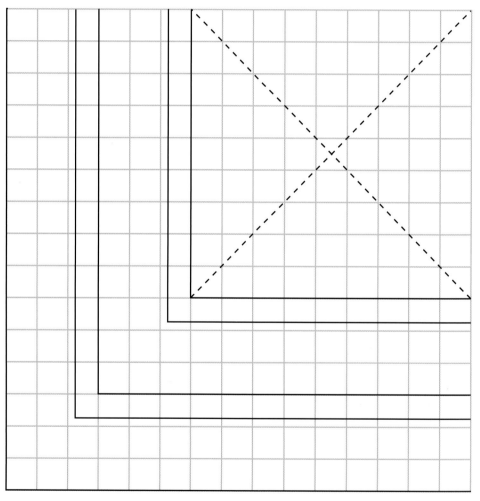

1 SQUARE = 2 INCHES

See diagram *below.*

B **After your design is in place**, start painting the diamonds. Put a light "X" on each diamond that you want to be painted the darker color. Of the diamonds to be painted, tape off every other one. Keep the drawn lines just inside the tape so they'll be painted over. Roll the paint on with a 4-inch roller, being careful not to roll outside the tape. Re-coat if necessary.

■ **Remove the tape**. Allow the first diamonds to dry thoroughly before you tape off and paint the remaining diamonds.

■ **Tape off the borders in the same way**. Touch up with a small artist's brush if necessary. Allow the floor to thoroughly dry. For durability, seal with two coats of satin polyurethane, allowing drying time between coats.

2

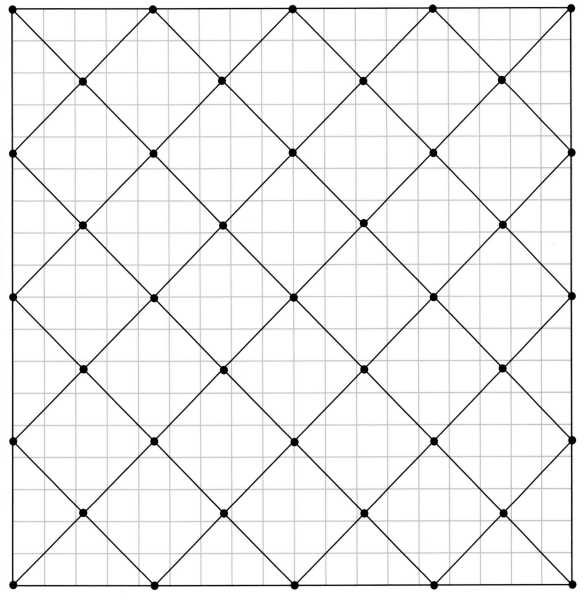

1 SQUARE = 4 INCHES

CONTRIBUTORS/RESOURCES

Pages 10-19 Decorative painting and styling: Wade Scherrer, Des Moines, Iowa; photography: Pete Krumhardt, Des Moines, Iowa.

Pages 20-35 Decorative painting: Wade Scherrer and Patty Kramer, Ames, Iowa; painting: Kerns Company, Des Moines, Iowa; styling: Wade Scherrer; photography: Pete Krumhardt; paint: The Home Depot: 800/553-3199.

Pages 36-37 Decorative painting: Wade Scherrer and Patty Kramer; photography: Pete Krumhardt; paint: The Home Depot.

Page 38 Decorative painting: Brian Carter; Atlanta, Georgia; photography: Emily Minton, Atlanta, Georgia.

Pages 44-45 Decorative painting: Wade Scherrer and Patty Kramer; photography: Pete Krumhardt.

Page 49 (Upper left) photography: Ross Chapple.

Page 56 Decorative painting: Brian Carter; photography: Emily Minton.

Page 57 Photography: Gordon Beall, Chevy Chase, Maryland.

Pages 58-59 Decorative painting: Brian Carter; photography: Emily Minton.

Page 64 Photography: Gordon Beall.

Page 69 (Lower right) Photography: Gordon Beall.

Pages 72-73 Decorative painting: Brian Carter; photography: Emily Minton.

Page 75 (Upper right) photography: James Yochum, Sawyer, Michigan/Tuscon, Arizona; (lower left) photography: Pete Krumhardt.

Pages 76, 79 Photography: Gordon Beall.

Page 80 (Upper left) photography: James Yochum; (lower left) photography: Pete Krumhardt.

Page 82 (Upper right) Gordon Beall.

Page 83 Design: Urban Country, Bethesda, Maryland; photography: Gordon Beall.

Page 84-85, Page 96 (Lower right) decorative painting: Brian Carter; photography: Emily Minton.

Page 100 (Right) photography: James Yochum.

Pages 101-103 Photography: Gordon Beall.

Pages 108-156 (Step-by-step techniques) decorative painting: Wade Scherrer and Patty Kramer; photography: Pete Krumhardt; paint: The Home Depot.

U.S. UNITS TO METRIC EQUIVALENTS

To Convert From	Multiply By	To Get
Inches	25.4	Millimeters (mm)
Inches	2.54	Centimeters (cm)
Feet	30.48	Centimeters (cm)
Feet	0.3048	Meters (m)

METRIC UNITS TO U.S. EQUIVALENTS

To Convert From	Multiply By	To Get
Millimeters	0.0394	Inches
Centimeters	0.3937	Inches
Centimeters	0.0328	Feet
Meters	3.2808	Feet